"Although I have known David Ireland only a relatively short period of time, each time we are together he stirs up something good inside of me. After reading this book, you will finish the final page, close the back cover, and feel something good taking up residence inside you. Permanently!"

Bill Hybels, senior pastor, Willow Creek Community Church and Willow Creek Association

"The founder of my tribe (John Wesley) likes to say that 'happiness is holiness.' David Ireland gets to the bottom of those all-important 'habits' of holiness that birth the only life that can both satisfy and serve."

Leonard Sweet, author, *Summoned to Lead*

"The information and technology age has brought us many great advancements and achievements in business and culture. Although the world is experiencing great change, it seems that insecurity and instability are the order of the day. Our personal lives are overwhelmed with decisions, stress, and issues that rob us of our peace of mind. To know God and to not know the peace he promises is frustrating and depressing at best. Frustrated and depressed people feel emotionally powerless.

"In *Secrets of a Satisfying Life*, Dr. Ireland helps us to get our power back! As I read the book, I felt as though some of my own burdens were being lifted off of my shoulders. Dr. Ireland shows us that we don't have to be under the circumstances of life but can find hope and happiness in spite of the circumstances of life. This is not some lightweight, feel-good book. Neither is it a deep analytical thesis on life's hidden meaning. However, this is indeed a book for those who want to get to the heart of the matter, see their life in the light of God's perspective, and begin living a real, joyful, satisfying life. Real life, real solutions, real results. If there is too much stuff weighing you down, then you need to read this book!"

Alvin Slaughter, recording artist; speaker; entrepreneur

"In the height of tsunamis, hurricanes, earthquakes, and other shakings, David Ireland shows biblical principles to give you peace and happiness. This is a must-read for everyone!"

Ché Ahn, author; pastor, Harvest Rock Church

"David Ireland takes the mask off of having a satisfying life. As Christians, we learn about joy but don't really understand how to be happy. *Secrets of a Satisfying Life* candidly shares experiences that led the author to be unhappy and unfulfilled. This book gives away some great secrets in order to gain a life that's worth living."

Bishop Harry R. Jackson, Jr., senior pastor, Hope Christian Church; chairman, High Impact Leadership Coalition

"Because life is full of stress, it is refreshing to read *Secrets of a Satisfying Life*. In his new book, David Ireland introduces us to a new level of freedom and happiness. He inspires us to enjoy the abundant life Christ provides in the midst of our present circumstances. By using his own personal experience and time-proven biblical principles, David enables the reader to lay hold of life-changing principles."

Rev. Paul Johansson, president, Elim Bible Institute

"Dr. David Ireland's insightful words blend the practical realities of life with spiritual principles of success to lay out clear steps to living the 'abundant life' that Jesus talked about. The truths that he shares with both wit and wisdom offer keys to unlocking the secret of Kingdom reality, encouraging all of us that a lifestyle lived God's way not only fulfills us but is one of the greatest witnesses we have!"

Robert Stearns, executive director, Eagles' Wings

secrets

of a satisfying life

DISCOVER THE HABITS
OF HAPPY PEOPLE

DAVID D. IRELAND, PH.D.

BakerBooks

Grand Rapids, Michigan

© 2006 by David D. Ireland, Ph.D.

Published by Baker Books
a division of Baker Publishing Group
P.O. Box 6287, Grand Rapids, MI 49516-6287
www.bakerbooks.com

Second printing, October 2006

Printed in the United States of America

Library of Congress Cataloging-in-Publication Data
Ireland, David, 1961–
    Secrets of a satisfying life : discover the habits of happy people / David D. Ireland.
        p.   cm.
    Includes bibliographical references.
    ISBN 10: 0-8010-6546-1 (pbk.)
    ISBN 978-0-8010-6546-0 (pbk.)
    1. Happiness—Religious aspects—Christianity. 2. Contentment—Religious aspects—Christianity. I. Title.
BV4647.J68174 2006
248.4—dc22   2005027485

contents

introduction

THE SEARCH FOR HAPPINESS

In an interview a few years back, Madonna—the multimillionaire pop star who has made a career of self-indulgent behavior—was asked, "Are you happy?" Her response was, "I don't even know anybody who is happy!"[1]

Happiness is a commodity Americans pursue as if it is part of our patriotic duty. The Declaration of Independence cites "the pursuit of happiness" as an inalienable right from God, and we aggressively seek this ideal in both our private and our public endeavors.

The Portrait of a Happy Man

You should have seen me on a recent family vacation. I was so happy sitting on my lounge chair under a coconut tree on the island of Puerto Rico. The sands were white, the birds of paradise were singing melodiously, and the tranquil breezes of the Atlantic Ocean blew gently across my face. My wife, Marlinda, was caressing my hand in hers. My biggest problem was deciding if I should reach for the tall glass of virgin piña colada or the juicy beach book lying next to me. If the legendary American artist Norman Rockwell had seen me, he would have painted my portrait and labeled it "The Happy Man." Then a frightening thought occurred to me: I could not make the moment last forever. But for that moment, I felt I was perfectly happy. This idyllic scene is the kind of image most people have in their minds when they think about happiness.

In general, how happy would you say you are—very happy, fairly happy, or not happy? The American Institute of Public Opinion has used this question for the past thirty years to measure people's state of happiness. Over that period of time, an average of 20 percent of Americans answered "very happy" to this routine question. The scientific reliability of this survey has undergone a lot of scrutiny. Behavioral scientists are skeptical of the survey because so many people's answers changed when they were re-interviewed one month later. In other words, people's levels of happiness varied within the short span of thirty days according to changes in their perspectives or circumstances. I would venture a guess that these interviewees discovered that what appeared to bring happiness later proved to be a mirage.

Happiness seems to be almost as hard to pin down as trying to win at the shell game. If you have ever ventured into one of the megacities of the world, you may have seen a shyster with a shell table. The game consists of three shells and a marble. The object is for a daring person to wager that he can pick out which shell the marble is under. The hustler invites the uninitiated into a game by staging a loss with an earlier gambler—someone planted in the audience as a winner. Unbeknownst to the passerby who stops to gawk at city life, the spider has spun a trap for the fly. The passerby sees an opportunity for "easy money" and accepts the shyster's challenge. He places a marble under a shell and shuffles the shells around quickly and skillfully. As the shells come to a stop, the gambler is asked to point to the shell that covers the marble. The gambler confidently points to the shell he believes is masking the marble. The hustler lifts the shell, and to the passerby's surprise, the marble is not where he thought it was. The shyster picks up another shell and shows the marble. The money exchanges hands, and another victim has been masterfully hustled.

Like the shell game's victim, most people are confident that happiness lies behind the next job, the next relationship, or the next experience, but they walk away disappointed when what they expect does not appear. Not only does the pursuit of happiness appear to be a futile endeavor, but the object that is supposed to bring happiness also seems to be always changing. This is one of the reasons that researchers receive different responses to the same questions after just a month's time.

The Pursuit of Happiness

Pursuing happiness is one thing; catching it is another. This emotionally charged quest for happiness reminds me of the story about an old dog that saw a younger dog chasing its tail.

"Why are you chasing your tail so?" the older dog asked.

The younger dog answered, "I have mastered philosophy; I have solved the problems of the universe which no dog before me has rightly solved. I have learned that the best thing for a dog is happiness and that happiness is my tail. Therefore, I am chasing it, and when I catch it, I shall have happiness."

"My son," answered the old dog, "I too have paid attention to the problems of the universe in my weak way, and I have formed some opinions. I too have judged that happiness is a fine thing for a dog and that happiness is in my tail. But I have noticed that when I chase after it, it keeps running away from me, but when I go about my business, it comes after me."

The older dog offered the young dog a wise lesson on the pursuit of happiness. Likewise, I believe that we can improve our satisfaction with life by studying the habits of happy people. Scientists spend most of their time carefully studying human disorders, seeking to find a remedy. My approach is just the opposite. By studying the healthy things that happy people are doing, we can discover a prescription for happiness. We will examine the common routines of happy people. Similar to the way a bank trains its tellers to spot counterfeit money by pointing out the distinct traits of authentic currency, we will study the habits of happy people so that we can quickly reject counterfeit sources of happiness in our lives. The real discovery, however, will be an ability to identify and implement the habits of happy people.

The Roadmap to Happiness

As your coach, I'd like to help you reach three goals through this book, namely: (1) to discover the habits of happiness; (2) to learn how to practice the habits of happiness; and, (3) to learn to laugh at yourself.

Discover the Habits of Happiness

First, I want to share in down-to-earth, practical terms the discoveries on happiness unearthed by psychologists and behavioral scientists. These discoveries tell us that we can form habits that create happiness. For example, a study by Bernard Rimland, director of the Institute for Child Behavior Research, concludes that "The happiest people are those who help others." Each person involved in the study was asked to list ten people he or she knew best and to label them as *happy* or *not happy*. Then they were asked to go through the list again and label each one as *selfish* or *unselfish* using the following definition of *selfishness*: "a stable tendency to devote one's time and resources to one's own interests and welfare—an unwillingness to inconvenience oneself for others."[2] In categorizing the results, Rimland found that all of the people labeled *happy* were also labeled *unselfish*. He wrote that those "whose activities are devoted to bringing themselves happiness ... are far less likely to be happy than those whose efforts are devoted to making others happy."[3]

Happiness increases by involving yourself in activities that support others. This is a principle that anyone can use to improve his or her personal state of happiness. It is the goal of this book to bring discoveries like this to your attention so that you can personally benefit from them.

Practice the Habits of Happiness

The second aim of this book is to provide you with examples of happy people who exercise particular habits and recognize them as the reason for their happiness. Dr. Viktor Frankl, author of *Man's Search for Meaning*, is an example of a man who found happiness though he suffered severely at the hands of brutal men. He was imprisoned by the Nazis during World War II because he was Jewish. His wife, his children, and his parents were all killed in the Holocaust. The gestapo stripped him of all his clothing and cut away his wedding band. As he stood there naked, Frankl said to himself, "You can take away my wife, you can take away my children, you can strip me of my clothes and my freedom, but there is one thing no person can *ever* take away from me—and that is my freedom to choose how I will react to what happens to me!"[4] You will discover that even under the most difficult circumstances, happiness is a choice that can transform our tragedies into triumph.

Learn to Laugh at Yourself

The third goal of this book is to help you lighten up and laugh.

As Reverend Jones walked through the poorest streets of Calcutta, he happened to see a number of young boys huddled around a little puppy and screaming at each other. The preacher walked hurriedly over to the boys to see if he could be of assistance. As he drew near, the boys quieted down a bit out of respect for the minister. Reverend Jones asked, "Boys, what's all the shouting about?"

The ringleader replied, "We found this puppy and each of us wants it for himself. We decided that whoever tells the biggest lie gets to keep the puppy."

Reverend Jones had heard enough; he launched into a fifteen-minute sermon on the ills of lying. As he was completing his moving sermon, he said, "Boys, when I was your age, we never played games like this."

The ringleader hung his head and said, "Give him the puppy."

The boys thought that the minister's words about not playing childhood games like theirs was the biggest lie they had heard. And based on the rules of the game, the puppy had to be given to him.

According to the Association for Applied and Therapeutic Humor, people who know how to laugh at life's awkward situations and even at themselves are far happier than those who don't.[5] As you read through the pages of this book, I hope that you experience some "Aha!" moments as you learn new ways of transforming your life. Enjoy the book. Be happy!

1

the value of perspective

Just as the old dog offered the younger dog a new perspective concerning his approach to pursuing happiness, I am urging you to examine your perspective on the matter. You must create a healthy perspective about happiness before attempting to model the habits of happy people. Your perspective makes all the difference in the world. Your perspective means your point of view, the way you see and interpret life around you.

One minister had established a time during his Sunday service when the children all marched past the pulpit, singing a recessional hymn, just before going into their Sunday school classrooms.

"For me, as their pastor," he reflected, "one of the high points of the service was the privilege of catching a smile from each child and giving one in return. I tried never to miss a single one, but one day apparently I failed. A little, curly-haired four-year-old ran out of the procession and threw herself into the arms of her mother, sobbing as though her heart was broken," he said. "After the service I sought out the mother. She said that when she had quieted the little one and asked why she had cried, she received this pathetic answer: 'I smiled at God, but he didn't smile back to me!' For her I stood for God. I had failed with my smile, and the world went dark."[1] This minister found out in a rather awkward way that people's perspectives are their realities.

I made a similar discovery several years ago while working in the field of consulting engineering. Much of my job had to do with designing wastewater treatment systems and writing reports about the building and maintenance of new technology. I started having terrible headaches that lasted from morning to evening each day. Since I wear glasses, I thought maybe I needed a new prescription due to excessive computer work or my getting older.

I scheduled an appointment with my optometrist, and he gave me a thorough eye exam. "Nothing is wrong with your eyes or the prescription of your lenses," he concluded. "Perhaps your company is working you too hard," he added. "It's probably the stress of the job and the amount of reading you're doing, compounded by the excessive hours you spend staring at the computer screen." Instantly I felt myself becoming angry at what my job was doing to me. *My boss is a slave driver. He's trying to kill me*, I thought.

Before leaving the optometrist's office, I decided to have the optician tighten some loose screws in my glasses. As he adjusted the screws, he said to me, "Sir, do you realize that the frame of your glasses is bent?"

"No," I said.

"Have you been having headaches?" he asked. My eyes shot open as my head bobbed up and down to say yes. I couldn't believe it. I was about to leave the eyeglass store angry at my boss, the company, and every one of my assignments, all because my glasses were out of alignment.

Some have said, "perspective is reality." In other words, the perspective you have, whether right or wrong, establishes your reality. The way you see others, the way you feel emotionally, the way you interpret the world around you, and even the judgments you make are all shaped by your perspective. As a result, when you approach the subject of happiness, you must continually reevaluate your perspective to ensure that it is accurate. If it is not, you are likely to operate under wrong assumptions, which may negatively affect your mood, judgments, emotions, and outlook on life. In a sense, your perspective—not your situation—may be the cause of your unhappiness. Therefore, performing regular perspective checks is an important exercise.

Checking Your Perspective

Oftentimes we allow our emotions to get out of control simply because we do not take the time to assess the accuracy of our perspectives. A perspective is formed with every experience. And if we are not careful, our reactions to crises, problems, or uncomfortable interactions with others can bring about a whole host of thoughts that generate a faulty perspective. This is precisely why Daniel Goleman in his popular book *Working with Emotional Intelligence* emphasizes the point that emotional awareness is one of the foundational skills vital to becoming emotionally intelligent.[2] Emotional intelligence is a relatively new phrase that acknowledges that one can gain knowledge about people and relationships from the emotions present in the process of relating to one another. Emotional awareness simply means the ability to recognize your emotions and their effects. The more in tune you are to your emotions and their potential to give you an incorrect perspective, the more emotionally intelligent and happier you will be.

Abraham Lincoln made it a practice never to show his anger in public. He felt that it was important to avoid the possible relational conflicts angry outbursts can bring, particularly when created by the forming of a hasty perspective. Instead, he would express his thoughts in a lengthy letter to the erring party. Gary McIntosh, a student of Lincoln's leadership style, writes, "He would then hang on to the letter and read it periodically until the anger subsided, finally disposing of it, having never mailed it. It was in this way that he could vent his feelings without giving needless offense to others, which would create barriers to his leadership."[3] Lincoln's mastery of checking his perspective, which positively affected his behavior, is one of the ways he maintained self-control and a pleasant state of mind and also earned his followers' respect.

Lincoln's habit in dealing with conflict points to the value of inner-directed behavior. You can learn to master a healthy perspective by applying a four-point approach to handling difficulties. Ask yourself:

1. Am I responding impulsively?
2. Is this the worst thing that can happen to me?
3. What do I want my future to look like?
4. How can I establish a strategy for happiness as part of the overall solution?

These four points can be adjusted and personalized to aid you in establishing the most accurate perspectives possible. The bottom line, however, is finding a way to evaluate how you look at things. You cannot achieve happiness if you are using wrong evaluations. Our emotions are usually connected to our interpretations, which are created from the perspectives we form. The four checkpoints provide a safeguard to help you develop a healthy perspective that can lead to happiness. Let's look at each one.

Am I Responding Impulsively?

About four years ago on April 1—we Americans call this day April Fools' Day—my daughter Danielle pulled one over on me. On April Fools' Day, pranksters use practical jokes to trick or mislead a family member or friend into believing something that isn't true. I was engrossed in writing a business plan and completely oblivious that it was April Fools' Day.

At school that day, Danielle and the rest of her teenage friends played practical jokes on one another and anyone else they could find. When she came home, she said to me with a grave expression on her face, "Dad, I was expelled from school today." Because I have stressed the value of a good education to both my daughters, I instantly became enraged on the inside. But knowing that exploding would not be the best way to handle this, I paced back and forth before responding to her statement. When I stopped and was about to give a response to her announcement, she laughed and said, "Ha, ha, ha, April Fools—I was just joking!" She then went into the kitchen to get a snack.

Little did she know what had been churning inside me. I was about to say something I should not have—an impulsive comment was about to fly out of my mouth. Although she had simply pulled a fast one on me, my anger did not subside for another half hour. After I calmed down, I realized how destructive an impulsive response to bad news can be.

---

the value of perspective

Establish a rule that bad news cannot be responded to impulsively, and you will find a wealth of satisfaction. A levelheaded response will help you maintain a positive state of mind.

Is This the Worst Thing That Can Happen to Me?

This question brings to fore a long-term perspective regarding bad news or painful circumstances. The difficulty that confronts you should be viewed in light of your entire life, so that you ask yourself, "Is this bad situation the worst thing that can happen over the span of my life?" The answer is almost always no. And the no answer will help you to formulate a healthy perspective and safeguard your emotional state. This intellectual filter becomes a checkpoint to help you achieve and maintain a state of happiness.

Aleksandr Solzhenitsyn wrote, "It was only when I lay there on rotting prison straw that I sensed within myself the first stirrings of good. Gradually, it was disclosed to me that the line separating good and evil passes not through states, nor between classes, nor between political parties either—but right through every human heart—and through human hearts. . . . I nourished my soul there, and I say without hesitation: Bless you, prison, for having been in my life."[4] These words convey Solzhenitsyn's discovery that he alone had power over his perspective concerning his imprisonment in a Soviet labor camp. And if a healthy perspective can be controlled in such a horrendous situation as a concentration camp, shouldn't we be able to implement this checkpoint all the more in lesser situations? Ultimately, you alone must answer the question, *Is this the worst thing that can happen to me?* Your answer will affect your perspective on happiness.

secrets of a satisfying life

What Do I Want My Future to Look Like?

Before you respond to a crisis, ask yourself this important question: *What do I want my future to look like?* This question forces you to rethink the actions that you may be tempted to take during difficult times. Your present state of happiness or the lack thereof reflects the choices and decisions you made yesterday. And because thoughts of the future may not have been factored into your past decisions, you are now reaping what you've sown. If you want to end the perpetual cycle of pain or unhappiness, placing a high priority on the future can make a huge difference.

I recently performed the nuptials for a couple that pulled out all the stops for their wedding day. Two stretch limousines—one a Mercedes Benz and one a Rolls Royce—were parked in front of the church. Other features of this gala included rare flowers, upscale furnishings, a mini orchestra, a choir, and expensive favors for the nearly seven hundred guests. The ceremony alone must have cost about $50,000, in addition to the reception hall, catered food, and two-week honeymoon to a Caribbean island. Though both the bride and the groom are professionals, they are not millionaires or the children of well-to-do parents. And while I enjoyed the sumptuous food and appreciated the extravagant pampering, I could not stop thinking about how this couple had foolishly spent close to $100,000 in a single day. Even though it was their wedding day, I was concerned about how little this couple had invested in planning their marriage. Like so many people, they were only thinking about the moment and not about the future.

You safeguard your happiness when you value your future. Regularly ask yourself the question *What do I want my future to look like?* The answer will force you to take an active role today in preparing for tomorrow's happiness.

If you want to create a healthy perspective that can lead to a state of happiness, the strategy you formulate must include a moral guideline for living. The code you create and ultimately live by will prevent such emotional baggage as guilt, regret, and second-guessing.

God implemented such a strategy to guide the behavior of the Jewish people. And today the Ten Commandments (Exod. 20:1–17) still serve as a moral compass in the Judeo-Christian community. God's intent was to provide a moral code that would safeguard the newfound freedom and happiness the Israelites gained after escaping Egypt. Changing their perspectives from the previous lifestyle of downtrodden slaves would require a new strategy if freedom and happiness are to be sought after. However, the Jews, like many people today, reversed God's commandments because they thought that the opposite of what he prescribed would give them happiness. Often people rewrite the Ten Commandments in this kind of upside-down fashion:

Ten Commandments of Happiness

1. You shall have no other gods before me . . . *unless* it makes you unhappy.
2. You shall not make for yourself an idol . . . *unless* it makes you unhappy.
3. You shall not misuse the name of the Lord your God . . . *unless* it makes you unhappy.
4. Remember the Sabbath day by keeping it holy . . . *unless* it makes you unhappy.
5. Honor your father and your mother . . . *unless* it makes you unhappy.

6. You shall not commit murder ... *unless* it makes you unhappy.
7. You shall not commit adultery ... *unless* it makes you unhappy.
8. You shall not steal ... *unless* it makes you unhappy.
9. You shall not give false testimony against your neighbor ... *unless* it makes you unhappy.
10. You shall not covet your neighbor's house, or wife, or anything that belongs to your neighbor ... *unless* it makes you unhappy.

The best approach to happiness is to follow the Commandments the way they were originally given in Exodus 20.

The four checkpoints I have outlined here have enabled me to develop and maintain a healthy and accurate perspective on life. And the added bonus is that they are based on the Bible. As Scripture says, "How can a young man keep his way pure? By living according to your [God's] word" (Ps. 119:9). This and other foundational truths from Scripture create the necessary mental filters to help purify how we look at what happens to us. When we do this, God is honored in our assessments. In the case of the young man referenced in this verse, his life is kept pure and honorable before God because he allows the Bible to have a strong and final control over his actions and opinions. In other words, what God thinks and decides about a matter is what the young man seeks to adopt as his own view. He is in essence demonstrating that a partnership with God helps him achieve personal satisfaction.

What Is Happiness?

Remember Madonna's response that she doesn't even know anyone who is happy? Well, that shouldn't surprise you. The old cliché rings true: money cannot buy happiness. Money and fame coupled with an outlandish, decadent lifestyle didn't buy Madonna happiness. Happiness is not subject to your wealth, social status, race, or educational level. Happiness does not elude some people due to their low level on the social ladder, nor is it guaranteed to others because of their high achievements. The common definition of happiness applies to all; happiness means having a sense of personal satisfaction. Given that simple definition, we can reasonably conclude that everyone and anyone should be able to live in a state of happiness.

As a minister, I am continually looking for new ways of helping people find happiness. Despite all of our advances in medicine and psychology, I find that the Bible provides the simplest and most valuable direction. In a letter written by the apostle Paul during his imprisonment in a Roman jail, he reveals that he has *learned* to be happy despite his circumstances: "I know what it is to be in need, and I know what it is to have plenty. I have learned the secret of being content in any and every situation, whether well fed or hungry, whether living in plenty or in want" (Phil. 4:12). In commenting on this verse, the eminent New Testament Greek scholar Jac Müeller writes, "He [Paul] *has learned* . . . in the school of life, and now he *knows* by virtue of his own experience how to be abased by need and want and adverse circumstances, and how to be provided for in an abundant way."[5] Paul's life experiences became the laboratory where the self-discovery of happiness occurred.

The Secret to Happiness Can Be Discovered

When Paul wrote to the church at Philippi, he was on trial for being a missionary of Christianity. He was facing a death sentence, albeit on trumped-up charges. He had every reason to be angry, bitter, and unhappy. Yet he confidently affirmed that he was "content," which means that he was personally satisfied. Although Paul was quite obviously somewhere he did not deserve to be and was being held against his will, he wrote that his personal satisfaction was not determined by his situation. Rather, it was unshaken because he had learned the secret of being content.

Two important points are gleaned from his statement: (1) happiness has very little to do with circumstance and more to do with perspective; and, (2) the secret of personal satisfaction can be learned.

Are You a Thermostat or a Thermometer?

Paul's outlook on life functioned the way a thermostat in your home works, rather than the way a thermometer operates. Sadly, most of our attitudes work like thermometers. In most homes you'll find a thermostat containing a thermometer. Although these words sound alike, the functions of the two devices are different. The thermostat regulates the temperature of the house, while the thermometer simply displays the temperature. If I want to lower or raise the house's temperature, I go over to the thermostat and press the button up or down. If I simply want to learn the temperature inside the house, I glance at the thermometer to see how many degrees it is in the house.

Paul was not oblivious to his dreary setting and unlawful imprisonment. Neither was he unaware of the horrible circumstances he was facing. He simply adjusted his thermostat—set his emotional temperature—to a comfortable setting, one of personal satisfaction. Perhaps someone else in the same situation would have turned his or her emotional thermostat to the setting called "anger" or "sadness" or "out of control," and this behavior would have been displayed on their personal thermometer for others to experience. Some people let the complex challenges they face control their emotional temperature. But if you let a predetermined thermostat set the standard, you will hold steady toward joy, optimism, or inner peace.

Paul was able to take charge of his feelings and perspective because, he said, he had learned the secret of being content. The phrase *learned the secret* implies that Paul took deliberate action that provided positive results over time and with use. Similarly, if you observe a really happy man, you will not find him searching for happiness as if it were the missing coin from a valued coin collection. Rather, you will find him building a boat, writing a symphony, educating his son, growing double dahlias in his garden, or looking for another masterpiece to add to his art collection. The actions or habits that he has developed over time have proven to be the secret to achieving personal satisfaction.

Some who have unsuccessfully attempted to crack the code to happiness have mistakenly equated positive thinking with happiness. But these two states are not the same. A man in a local supermarket was pushing a shopping cart that held, among other things, a screaming baby. As the man proceeded along the aisles, he kept repeating softly, "Keep calm, George. Don't get excited, George. Don't get angry, George. Don't yell, George."

A lady watching with admiration said to the man, "You are certainly to be commended for your patience in trying to quiet little George."

"Lady," he declared, "*I'm* George."

Thinking yourself happy does not make you happy any more than thinking yourself calm does.

Learning Habits of Happiness

A habit is a tendency or inclination that is either purposely or involuntarily adopted over time. Happy people have embraced consistent conduct and psychological responses to life that keep them feeling satisfied. According to sociologists Drs. William J. Cousins and Paul Oren of Yale University, a habit can also be defined as "the repetition of successful responses to a particular need."[6] Habits of happy people are deliberate responses that have successfully proven to meet their personal emotional needs. These habitual responses can be taught and learned in the same way that coaches train their players or the way mentors teach their craft to their protégés. My aim is to become your happiness coach by teaching you the habits that happy people routinely employ.

Before you begin learning new habits, however, let's determine where you are right now. How satisfied are you with your life? The Satisfaction With Life Scale (SWLS) that follows was developed by behavioral scientists. It does not measure satisfaction with specific areas such as health and finances. It allows you to consider, in a general sense, how the things that concern you contribute to your overall satisfaction or lack thereof. Honestly indicate your agreement with each of the five statements below by placing a check mark next to the number which best communicates how you feel about the statement.

1. In most ways my life is close to my ideal.
_____ 1. strongly disagree   _____ 5. slightly agree
_____ 2. disagree   _____ 6. agree
_____ 3. slightly disagree   _____ 7. strongly agree
_____ 4. neither agree or disagree

2. The conditions of my life are excellent.

_____ 1. strongly disagree   _____5. slightly agree

_____ 2. disagree   _____6. agree

_____ 3. slightly disagree   _____7. strongly agree

_____ 4. neither agree or disagree

3. I am satisfied with my life.

_____ 1. strongly disagree   _____5. slightly agree

_____ 2. disagree   _____6. agree

_____ 3. slightly disagree   _____7. strongly agree

_____ 4. neither agree or disagree

4. So far I have gotten the important things I want in life.

_____ 1. strongly disagree   _____5. slightly agree

_____ 2. disagree   _____6. agree

_____ 3. slightly disagree   _____7. strongly agree

_____ 4. neither agree or disagree

5. If I could live my life over, I would change almost nothing.

_____ 1. strongly disagree   _____5. slightly agree

_____ 2. disagree   _____6. agree

_____ 3. slightly disagree   _____7. strongly agree

_____ 4. neither agree or disagree

After you have answered all five questions, total your overall score by adding the numbers next to each of the five choices selected. For example, if for question #1 you checked "slightly disagree," your score for that particular question would be 3 points. Add up all five numbers to get your overall score. The total number of points will help you determine your personal level of satisfaction with life.

Overall scores for the Satisfaction With Life Scale are interpreted in terms of absolute and relative satisfaction with life. If your score totals in the range of 31–35, you are *extremely satisfied* with your life. If you scored 26–30, you are *satisfied* with your life. If your score is 21–25, you are *slightly satisfied*, and if your score is 20, you are in a *neutral* position, which means that you are *equally satisfied and dissatisfied* with your life. A score of 15–19 means that you are *slightly dissatisfied* with your life; 10–14 represents *dissatisfied*; and 5–9 indicates that you are *extremely dissatisfied* with your life.

If you didn't score in the *extremely satisfied* category, don't worry. Keep reading and you will discover workable answers to help you achieve a satisfying life.

2

happy habits

We cannot choose to be born, and we cannot opt out of death. Birth and death are constants for all people. But we can choose *how* to live. Some people have chosen to live as pessimists, finding nothing but problems with life, while others have decided to become optimists, noticing only positive things amidst life's strange moments. The choice of perspective is yours to make. Happiness is also a choice. A happy outlook on life is not some mantra prescribed by the New Age gurus. Its benefits are supported by the research findings of behavioral scientists who have probed the habits of people who have demonstrated true happiness and satisfaction with life.

The habits of happy people are intentional responses that have proven to meet their need to manage life. These happy people did not start out knowing the habits that would bring them happiness; rather, they learned these responses along the way to finding a satisfying life. You can learn to lead a satisfying life by implementing these same workable principles, which can be developed into intentional habits. The first principle is making a deliberate choice to pursue the road that leads to a life of satisfaction.

I will explain some common habits which have been proven scientifically to deliver a measure of happiness and satisfaction. For instance, a groundbreaking study by professors Ed Denier and Martin Seligman showed that "very happy people were highly social, and had stronger romantic and other social relationships than less happy groups."[1] This observation supports the premise that if you're more extroverted, more agreeable, and have less hang-ups, you would be happier with yourself. Consequently you would be more of a social butterfly. Since the practices of taking regular outings, expressing love, and building relationships are habits of happy people, it doesn't take a leap of faith to believe that if unhappy or moderately happy people incorporated these practices, they would be a lot more satisfied with life and, therefore, much happier.

The Power of a Habit

By observing the practices and values of ordinary people, behavioral scientists have been able to define certain habits that characterize happy people. I will present this social data without the technical language of the research and will present these habits along with practical advice. My aim is to demystify happiness by showing you easy ways of developing the habits that have proven to bring satisfaction to others. The habits of happy people are best seen as intentional responses that have proven to meet their needs.

secrets of a satisfying life

First we must examine one negative habit: choosing to make excuses. My wife, Marlinda, told me for years that I was a workaholic. Her exact words were, "David, you need to stop putting in so many hours at the church office. You're not invincible. Everyone's pastoral emergency need not be attended to by you. You have a family." Although her words stung, I justified my behavior with the thought that the work needed to get done and I was the only person who could do it. And I had all of my excuses lined up to refute her claims. Yet over time the excuses became more and more complicated.

Happiness is a choice. Making excuses for one's unhappiness is also a choice. In Paul's written instructions to the church at Philippi, he shared this eye-opening perspective on life: "I have learned to be content whatever the circumstances. I know what it is to be in need, and I know what it is to have plenty. I have learned the secret of being content in any and every situation, whether well fed or hungry, whether living in plenty or in want. I can do everything through him [Jesus] who gives me strength" (Phil. 4:11–13).

What expectations of spiritual growth do you have for yourself as you read these pages? How often have you been to God, the supreme Judge, saying, "God, when are you going to hear my case and increase the quality of my life? When are you going to give me the help I need to become more successful in business or in my marriage?" Let me say that the answer to this question depends not on your ability to fathom God's timing but on *you*—on the intensity of your expectations that tomorrow your walk with God will be better than today's predicament and on your level of trust in him. God's response can come in any form he chooses. However, you'll have a greater probability of getting the boost you need as you seek to employ habits that lead to spiritual growth and satisfaction. In approaching the habits one ought to employ to yield a satisfying life, you must adopt the mind-set of a champion athlete, or what I call a spiritual champion.

Championing Spiritual Habits

An essential habit of spiritual champions can be found in the world of sports, as is vividly illustrated on the pages of the newspaper sports section every day. If you pay close attention to interviews with tennis stars Venus and Serena Williams, you can discern that these champions have a distinctive attitude—one that exudes confidence and certitude. Some people might say that these young women are proud, but I think that's a misreading. I believe that the Williams sisters demonstrate an attitude that's consistently reflected in the mind-set of champions: they're *expecting* to win.

You rarely hear a champion, whether in sports or business or any other field, say, "Well, tomorrow I think I'm going to lose." No, they pump themselves up with a winning attitude. I think this attitude stems from the fact that champions simply don't focus on being defeated. They radiate confidence, not defeatism. They expect that the gifts and discipline and attitude that have brought them this far will take them even farther in the next challenge.

I affirm that this attitude of confidence and the expectation of victory characterize spiritual champions too. This is not an approval of egotism or self-sufficiency. To the contrary, I'm saying that believers *depend* on the fact that their victory is assured by *the* Victor—*Christus Victor*, as Swedish theologian Gustav Aulen described Jesus.[2] Spiritual champions expect to be victorious because their Lord, the ultimate Champion, leads them to victory. Likewise, if you

secrets of a satisfying life

are going to succeed in learning and adopting the habits of happy people as part of your new lifestyle, you need a mind-set of expectation.

Remember how you anticipated your birthday or Christmas as a child? You may have thought about it for weeks. Your parents may have had to work hard to keep you from rummaging through the closet in search of hidden gifts. The prospects had you tingling with excitement.

In Luke 11:9–10, Jesus gives a picture of the expectation of spiritual champions. I want to cite it here with the dimension of promise and expectation in italics for emphasis:

> Ask and *it will be given* to you; seek and *you will find*; knock and *the door will be opened* to you. For everyone who asks *receives*; he who seeks *finds*; and to him who knocks, *the door will be opened*.

If we look at this well-known passage carefully, we can see that it holds the key to the problem we've all experienced when our expectations have been dampened . . . when the "doors" we pray to be opened seemed to stay shut.

The key lies in understanding the tense of the verbs used here. They are in the "present continuous imperative" tense of *koine* (or "common") Greek, the language of the New Testament. That fancy label simply means that verbs in that tense have an *ongoing* or *continuous* connotation. In this case Jesus is saying that instead of being disheartened when the doors of satisfaction in life don't immediately open for us, we are to *keep on asking, keep on seeking*, and *keep on knocking*.

In other words, spiritual champions don't give up easily in pursuing the object of their expectations. They know that God has his reasons when he postpones answers to prayer. Their expectations that he will inspire their quest for spiritual victories aren't dampened by the fact that he answers in his own good time.

If we allow setbacks in spiritual growth to discourage us, we too easily lapse into anxiety. This is what prompted the apostle Paul to write, "Do not be anxious about anything, but in everything, by prayer and petition, with thanksgiving, present your requests to God" (Phil. 4:6). This lack of anxiety is what I see in the Williams sisters and other champions in demanding fields. Their expectations are strong enough that they don't take every bump in the road toward their goal as a matter to worry about. Neither are you to take a bump in the road as a reason to stop learning how to practice these happy habits outlined herein.

As I write, one of the nation's best professional football teams has just lost a crucial game. From the start, the players seemed preoccupied, unfocused, and listless. Had I been the coach I would have stormed up and down the sidelines challenging my players with the most obvious question I can imagine: *Are you in the game or just watching?*

I am convinced that one of the most urgent needs of modern Christians is to maintain the sense that we are in a race or a contest. If you are a believer, you have enrolled in a competition. You gave up your right to be a mere spectator when you gave your life to Christ.

Despite what our consumer culture tells us, this competition is not to be the wealthiest or the smartest or to see who can wind up with the most toys. Nor are Christians competing against each other. Rather, we race toward the destiny God has carved out for us. We compete against the great adversary, Satan, rather than against others who are also in the race. Our goal is to live satisfying lives so that our lives can testify to God's leadership and goodness. Our hope is to see others experience the precious salvation for which Jesus died on Calvary's cross.

We also need to realize that the spiritual race is not a 60-yard dash. Rather, it's a marathon. The Christian walk is one of *longevity*, not of just a short burst of speed. Anyone can get out of the starting blocks with a burst of energy, but the question is where we will be 30 or 60 or maybe 100 yards down the track. The most fundamental aspect of learning how to employ these "happy habits" is that regardless of how long it takes you to learn the habits, you determine to keep moving toward the finish line—achieving a satisfied life.

Hungry for a Satisfying Life

Reinvent Yourself If Necessary

In her recent book *New Passages*, Gail Sheehy observes how many American adults around the ages of 35 to 45 are going into what she calls "middlescence."[3] They've been through *adol*escence (their teen years) and young adulthood, but as they approach middle age they seek a new start, a new lease on life, a fresh lift for the race—hence "middlescence."

That's why we see so many "second career" people. People in their fifties are now attending medical schools and seminaries. No matter how much salary they lose by leaving their present job, many "middlescent" people are switching careers because they value personal satisfaction more than money. Often they are doing this to resist the dead feeling that can come when you feel that in your present job you've become dissatisfied or closed to new ideas or change.

One factor behind this trend is that when people reach midlife, they can see things from a perspective they lacked in earlier years. Many "middlescent" people have come to deem important some things that they dismissed earlier as unimportant—job satisfaction instead of income, for example. Such people are willing to make financial sacrifices because they know they are in this race for the long haul. And living a satisfying life is more rewarding than job status or being the king (or queen) of the hill.

A typical American man who lives to age 60 will not die until around age 91. The typical American woman who reaches age 60 will live until about age 95. This means that when people reach ages 35 to 45, a new lease on life is important. They are actually seeking a second adult life to keep the spark, the fervency, that the long haul requires. Thus, reinventing oneself is usually the primary focus at this juncture in life. With a new outlook comes the search for new habits that will yield the satisfaction one craves.

The Search for Satisfaction

I think we all could use a little of this "middlescent" attitude, whatever our age. Even in my own career as a minister I see the danger of letting my work become "institutional" or dull instead of ever-new and challenging.

I began pastoring Christ Church when I was twenty-four. I was probably the youngest one in the congregation except for my wife, who is just a year younger than I am. Two weeks after the church began, our first child, Danielle, was born. So I grew up as a man, a father, and a pastor at Christ Church all at once.

Now I am in the second decade of my ministry at Christ Church. God has blessed us with growth, but that very growth carries with it the danger of institutionalism. I dare not fall into the trap of allowing the fresh enthusiasm of my earlier years of ministry to become dulled by "middle-aged professionalism." I need a constantly growing definition of ministry and a passionate concern for my own spiritual development as a leader. I need to have a renewed sense of the need to apply God's ever-fresh Word to every area of my life so that I may finish this race strong. This new perspective will also help me maintain a teachable spirit toward adopting life-altering habits that will help me achieve and maintain a satisfying life.

The little book of Jude has been a warning for me, as it is for every person seeking to grow. From a minister's perspective, it is a warning not to become "shepherds who feed only themselves" (Jude 12).

To avoid this trap, ministers (and everyone else for that matter) must be *intentional* about telling themselves, "Don't function in your walk with the Lord simply as a pastor or as a professional speaker. Don't just 'do your job.' Function in your walk with the Lord as an ongoing student of Jesus." Otherwise, we can easily succumb to the temptation of perceiving ourselves as professional teachers and forget that effective teaching is an in-the-trenches relationship with real people with real problems in the muck and mire of everyday life.

Everyone faces the temptation of "middle-aged" thinking, regardless of their age or proximity to societal trends. This is especially true in the case of those who have experienced some measure of success. We can get so used to our success that we build into our lifestyles various principles and familiar patterns that are necessary to maintain that success. But if we are not sensitive, these very patterns can degenerate into mere "mechanical" systems, rather than serving as a dynamic force that produces a satisfied life. If we have no real sense of passion to keep advancing in achieving a satisfying life, we can unconsciously become mere shells of the vital, Spirit-empowered disciple we used to be.

To quote again from the book of Jude, Christians must not become "clouds without rain" (v. 12). People living in drought-stricken sections of the world get excited when a cloud appears on the horizon, but they aren't really blessed until they get rain. And if we have experienced a measure of satisfaction with our lives, that is not cause enough to cease from exploring new ways to climb to the next rung on the ladder of a satisfying life.

We have all heard of people who used to enjoy leading a satisfying life but for some reason have stopped practicing the habits that got them to that point. They became so satisfied with their lives that they unconsciously slipped into a downward spiral of becoming lukewarm. These unfortunate examples should be warning enough for us not to become settled in our little bit of satisfaction but to keep moving upward through practicing happy habits. In so doing, we will glorify our God with a satisfying life that is achieved and maintained through his grace.

So one of the habits I urge you, as a modern Christian, to adopt and to hold as precious and dear is the habit of knowing that you are in a race and that you are in it for the long haul. You're not on the sidelines. You're not a spectator in a sporting competition. You're a competitor.

I want to underscore the fact that you're not competing against another person. As an individual Christian you are in a spiritual race against yourself, and you run toward the goal of being conformed to the image of Christ. It won't happen, however, if you don't see yourself as one who is in a race, one who intentionally and constantly subjects himself or herself to the disciplines, or the habits, of the spiritually successful person.

Spiritual Discipline

The apostle Paul draws from the world of sports to demonstrate the way to cultivate happy habits. He said, "Everyone who competes in the games goes into strict training. They do it to get a crown that will not last; but we do it to get a crown that will last forever" (1 Cor. 9:25). Paul is referring to the Isthmian games. Part of the rules of competing in the games was that participants had to go through a ten-month regimen of strict discipline and rigorous training. If you chose not to go through the training, you were removed or disqualified from competing.

A recent edition of the magazine *Runner's World* carried a picture of President George W. Bush on the cover. The magazine said that he is the fastest president—he runs a mile in about seven minutes. And the President says that if he, as the country's top leader, can get up and run, then anyone else can get up and run.[4] In other words, if he can find time to jog, certainly we who don't have that level of pressure or stress on our lives can find time to exercise. Habits take time to form. Give yourself over to the daily practice of the happy habits and over time you will see yourself evolving into a fully satisfied person.

Keep Your Eyes on the Prize

So much of running to cross the finish line Christ has set before us has to do with our motives, with the *why* of the race. Bear in mind *who you are*—Christ's servant called to run the race, not to compete with anyone else but to cross the line he has drawn for you up ahead. If your motivation is only to "keep up" with someone you admire, you may lose heart when you lag behind. If you fail to run at all, you risk spiritual anemia, apathy, and stagnation. Picture yourself as training for no one else but Christ. Achieving a satisfied life will not only help you but also enhance the attraction of the kingdom of God to people who don't know God.

Bear in mind also your role as part of the Christian community. You are called to do your part to keep yourself and others in the body of Christ from becoming anemic and apathetic. The church's immune system will not ward off disease and predators if its individual members are weak, undisciplined, and living unfulfilled lives. Believers cannot possibly remain mere spectators if they keep in mind Peter's stirring description of the body as "a chosen people, a royal priesthood, a holy nation, a people belonging to God, that you may declare the praises of him who called you out of darkness into his wonderful light" (1 Peter 2:9).

We must guard against many distractions. Think of the athletes and the crowd at a sporting event. The stands are filled with people rooting for one side or another. Sometimes the fans get so crazy and fanatical that they will boo a player who has missed a goal or made a bad play. Their screams and the anger in their words can really scar competitors if they allow the words to penetrate their hearts.

In the same way, we can easily be discouraged in our race toward a satisfying life by the "crowd noise." Yet we must not allow ourselves to be scarred by scorn and sharp words. We must be so disciplined that such would-be distractions fail to wrest our minds away from our firm intent to finish the race—and to finish strong.

We must be so well-disciplined that discouragement does not weaken our resolve. We must be trained in the Word of God, with our minds saturated with how *God* thinks of us instead of listening to our detractors—even when the detractor is an inner voice. You'll hear many reasons to say that you can't do it, you don't qualify, you don't belong, you don't have all of what it takes to lead a satisfying life. Each of us can come up with dozens of reasons why we should disqualify ourselves from being effective as husbands, wives, fathers, sons, brothers, mothers, daughters, or sisters. Yet despite such "reasons," in the end we must realize that the Bible calls us into a spiritual race—one that calls for using habits that lead to a fulfilled life.

It's time to learn the habits of happy people. Read on with the mind-set of a champion!

3

learning how to be satisfied

The cliché "You eat like a pig" is an oxymoron. Pigs have a built-in device that tells them when to stop eating, unlike us humans, who seldom recognize when our hunger is satisfied. Not knowing how to be satisfied is one of the greatest stumbling blocks to personal happiness. With such grandiose claims as "satisfaction guaranteed or your money back," marketing groups condition people to believe that this promise applies to every area of life, from toasters to marriage. Prenuptial agreements are a booming business, based on the same "satisfaction guaranteed or your money back" mind-set. More and more Americans are insisting, "If my marriage does not *make me* and *keep me* happy, I'm terminating this relationship and all of *my* property goes with me." This approach to happiness, however, is the very antithesis of what brings satisfaction.

A groundbreaking study by Allen Parducci, a behavioral psychologist on the faculty of the University of California at Los Angeles, indicates that learning how to be satisfied is a habit that happy people practice. This perspective is particularly refreshing because, according to Parducci, happy people typically experience the same range and degree of events as unhappy people.[1] In other words, happy people and unhappy people have the same number of bad experiences, family setbacks, painful dilemmas, and confusing turn of events. The difference is in their definitions and interpretations of positive and negative experiences.

The idea of thresholds can be used to explain this difference. A threshold is a level or a value above which something is true or acceptable. For instance, many students establish a B grade as a minimum grade for their happiness threshold. Although they aim for an A, they have adopted a healthy perspective that a B grade is still satisfactory in light of the rigor of the course work and their limited study time. Similarly, happy people have learned that far more things are acceptable than are unacceptable. Happy people attribute their happiness to the fact that they have learned the habit of using a lower threshold to determine what constitutes a positive experience. They do not need or expect everything to be perfect in order to be happy; they are content with a lower level. Their unhappy counterpart has a high threshold which cannot be attained all of the time and for every experience. But unhappy people keep these high expectations because they have concluded that this standard is where happiness lies. Anything falling below that benchmark, despite its positive components, renders them unhappy. This kind of perspective sets up unhappy people to remain unhappy despite all of the positive and wonderful things going on in their lives. Since an unrealistically high threshold is where an

secrets of a satisfying life

unhappy person thinks happiness lies, having four things go perfectly well will not produce happiness if the benchmark was set at five.

One day in a park zoo, a crowd watched a peacock spread its tail and show a dazzling plumage. The bird drew oohs and aahs from the people as it strutted regally about its pen. Then a dull-looking, brown-colored duck waddled between the peacock and the crowd. The peacock became angry and chased the duck back into a nearby pond. In the peacock's rage, its tail closed like a fan, and the bird seemed ugly. But the duck began swimming and diving gracefully in the pond and no longer seemed unattractive. Those who had been singing the praises of the peacock now loved the duck.

The peacock's threshold for happiness was to be the sole center of attention. Since the dull-colored duck began diverting some of the attention away from the peacock, the peacock could never be happy. Unhappy human beings are the same way. To avoid this trap of unconsciously setting an unrealistic threshold for happiness, you must understand and embrace the standards happy people use to establish their thresholds. Once you are aware of these factors, making them part of your daily regimen will become second nature over time.

Determining a Reasonable Threshold

The issue of threshold begs the question, *How do I determine what my minimum level of satisfaction is?* Solomon wrestled with the subject of happiness, and in the book of Ecclesiastes, a few of his time-tested findings have been preserved. The three answers Solomon establishes as reasonable thresholds for personal happiness are: (1) happiness is a choice; (2) happiness is the ability to find enjoyment out of life; and (3) happiness results from following your heart.

Happiness Is a Choice

In arriving at a threshold that yields satisfaction, you must make a choice—a decision as to how you will live with the outcome. Will you be satisfied? Or will you be upset and grouchy about the result? Happiness comes when you set a threshold of satisfaction that allows you to feel that an experience was positive. Unhappy people are reluctant to set such a limit because in their minds, happiness only occurs when the experience is perfect. Their happy counterparts find no difficulty, however, in drawing a positive conclusion from the same experience.

Solomon writes: "I know that there is nothing better for men than to be happy and do good while they live. That everyone may eat and drink, and find satisfaction in all his toil—this is the gift of God" (Eccles. 3:12–13). Solomon freely admits that all are in search of happiness. But rather than making happiness appear elusive and out of our reach, the prolific sage drops a big hint to our locating it: we must find satisfaction in all of our toil—our experiences. This is the very point that Parducci discovered in his research: happiness is determined largely by your evaluation of and conclusion regarding an experience. Your happiness threshold is established when you find an acceptable level of personal satisfaction. No one but you can conclude what is a reasonable threshold for you. You can be coached, but if you are not willing to enlarge your perspective as to what qualifies as a positive experience, all the coaching in the world will only result in creating frustration for you and your coach.

Solomon's definition of happiness was for a person to find satisfaction in all of his toil. In other words, satisfaction is not to be sought in the future. Nor is the quest for satisfaction to be put on hold until a better time or a better set of circumstances appears. Satisfaction is to be sought right now, in the middle of whatever is happening in your life. In adopting this newfound perspective, you are making a choice to be happy right in the midst of your present set of circumstances.

In teaching our daughter Danielle how to have a happier outlook on life, Marlinda and I constantly tell her, "Give a positive spin to the events rather than focusing so much attention on what went wrong." In other words, what went right? As parents we do not want to see our daughter, like so many adults, fall into the destructive pattern of only finding satisfaction *if* the experience was one hundred percent perfect. We can't attain perfection in every experience, all the time. I'm not suggesting that one should not hold a high standard of acceptability. What I'm lobbying for is a lifestyle practice that looks for the good in an experience and not just for the bad. I am also lobbying for the mind-set that satisfaction is to be sought in every situation and not just in the by-and-by.

After a trip to his dentist, one of the men in my congregation was experiencing persistent bleeding from a tooth extraction. As a result, he suddenly found out he had leukemia. Marco was thirty-five years old at the time, and he and Michele had been married for seven years and had three boys. News of this diagnosis brought their lives to a crashing halt. The medical fact made them come face-to-face with their mortality. It also forced them to rethink their lives and find answers that could carry them through this crisis.

Marco and Michele made a decision in that hospital room to look for a minimal threshold of satisfaction by putting a positive spin on this life-threatening circumstance. After a few hours of talking through Marco's illness and the potential tragedy of not seeing his three sons grow to become men, get married, and have families of their own, Marco saw clearly that at a minimum he wanted his family to know him as a man of God who knew how to enjoy any and every circumstance. That afternoon Marco accepted the fact that happiness was a choice and determined that even if the chemotherapy failed and divine healing did not occur, he was still going to be happy. A few days later, Marco and Michele's wedding anniversary found him in the hospital. Yet Marco's threshold of happiness was not affected. To help Marco maintain this newfound perspective, Michele surprised him by walking into his hospital room in her wedding gown. She wanted to renew their vows on their eighth wedding anniversary. As I watched the video that captured the event, I choked back tears as I saw Marco break into tears of joy as they exchanged their vows.

In a few months, Marco miraculously defeated the leukemia and rejoined his family in serving the Lord. He has held onto the practice of learning to be satisfied by making a choice to be happy.

Learn to Enjoy Life

The book of Ecclesiastes is a book about life. It captures King Solomon's philosophical quest to find answers that would quiet the turbulence of his soul-searching questions. Solomon's questions revolved around life, its meaning, and what outlook one ought to have on the seasons of life. Although Solomon was the richest man in the ancient world, his wealth could not give him happiness. Being sexually pleasured by his 700 wives and 300 concubines also did not satisfy his soul. He concluded that there is more to life than money, sex, and the pursuit of pleasure. Solomon wanted an outlook on life that could keep him feeling satisfied even when he was alone.

After searching for an answer, he realized that "it is good and proper for a man to eat and drink, and to find satisfaction in his toilsome labor under the sun during the few days of life God has given him—for this is his lot. Moreover, when God gives any man wealth and possessions, and enables him to enjoy them, to accept his lot and be happy in his work—this is a gift of God" (Eccles. 5:18–19). Finding satisfaction in life was the ingenious answer that ended the philosophical search of Solomon. Since life is filled with ordinary and necessary things such as eating, drinking, and working, the intention of God is for us to find satisfaction in these mundane events. Accepting this vantage point to life makes happiness more attainable and commonplace. This perspective ensures that happiness is not elusive, as many may believe. Happiness can and is to be found in the measure of satisfaction one can find in the normal activities of life.

Is Happiness for You?

For many people, Solomon's words are meaningless because deep down they believe that they will never have a satisfying life. The faulty thinking is, *Perhaps others can achieve it, but I cannot.* If this is your perspective, you couldn't be further from the truth. The promises of the Bible are for everyone. This includes you. The gifts of God, which include the ability to enjoy your assets, your work, and your life, are freely given to all. These gifts of God are part of the expression of his love for human beings, which includes you. The ability to enjoy life must be personally embraced without any hang-ups that may hold you back from this privilege.

I remember when I started college as an engineering student. One of the toughest courses I had to tackle was calculus—a high order of abstract math. I just couldn't grasp the concepts, and my grades reflected that reality. I began to think that there was nothing I could possibly do to earn a passing grade in calculus. This defeatist attitude remained inside me for weeks, although I knew that a passing grade was required to advance to my second year as an engineering student. My self-defeating attitude all changed one day when I read a little note my mother sent me. Although this occurred some twenty-five years ago, I remember it today as if it were just yesterday. The note read, "David, what man has done, man can do!" She wasn't aware of my struggles; no one was. But the note transformed my thinking. It gave me the perspective that if another person could tackle and understand calculus, so could I. The note put wind in my sail. I breezed through calculus and advanced to the sophomore level. I graduated within the four-year timeframe with my bachelor's degree in mechanical engineering.

Whatever your goal, the principle is the same when it comes to living a satisfying life: a satisfied life is available to everyone, including you.

Enjoy Life Today

The hard question that is vitally important to our discussion is, Can you begin to enjoy life if nothing in your life has changed? Most people are waiting to be happy. They are waiting for the baby to be born or waiting for the toddler to become potty trained. Others are waiting to buy the new house or waiting to move out of their parents' home.

Business people are waiting for that big contract to come in. The bottom line is, most people have taught themselves that happiness is only achieved when everything is perfect. Solomon teaches us that life is never perfect! We're always waiting for something or someone. But if we accept the outlook of the Scriptures, we need not wait in order to find satisfaction. Although life is filled with many mundane events, happiness is found in learning to enjoy life today!

Decide right now to stop complaining about your job, home, spouse, children, finances, or unfulfilled goals and start enjoying life. I'm not suggesting that you give up on your dreams or the desire for a more fulfilling relationship with those significant people in your life. Rather, I am encouraging you to establish a reasonable threshold to personal satisfaction by learning to enjoy life right now.

The Value of Realization

The turning point in Solomon's perspective on a satisfied life came when he *realized* that it is good to enjoy life (see Eccles. 5:18). Such a realization is like having the windshield of your car cleaned. You can see the road ahead without having to guess what is in your pathway. Similarly, when you realize that God intended for us to find satisfaction in the everyday things such as working, cooking, doing the laundry, or balancing the checkbook, your entire outlook can change. Suddenly the chore of cooking doesn't seem like a nuisance and your job is viewed as pleasurable rather than an annoying responsibility that only is carried out to make a buck.

Coming to this realization is not just the formalization of a new outlook. It is a gift of God. Solomon lobbies for this perspective to be part and parcel of the whole satisfaction piece. He writes, "when God gives any man wealth and possessions, and enables him to enjoy them, to accept his lot and be happy in his work—this is a gift of God" (Eccles. 5:19). Arriving at this new place of satisfaction includes the acceptance of one's lot, or one's state in life. It does not mean that you die to your aspirations and dreams. This outlook positions you to enjoy life now rather than postponing enjoyment for a future time when every aspect of your dreams is fulfilled.

A friend of mine recently had a stroke that affected his speech. After a few months of rehabilitation, Jim regained about 95 percent of his speaking abilities. Although I rejoiced in his recovery, another spectacular outcome of his near-death experience was that he was able to realize that life was given to be enjoyed. His adult son shared with me that he and his dad now had a great relationship because Jim had realized that every moment here on earth is precious. Nowadays they share small talk for hours on the telephone. But prior to the stroke every word spoken between them had to have a specific purpose. Solomon's observation is correct: "It is good and proper for a man to eat and drink, and to find satisfaction in his toilsome labor under the sun during the few days of life God has given him—for this is his lot" (Eccles. 5:18). Jim realized that pleasure could be found in simply speaking to his son about ordinary things.

Finding Satisfaction

Learning to enjoy life by finding satisfaction in the ordinary things of life may not come about without your taking a step of repentance toward God. Since accepting your lot and being happy in your work reflects acceptance of a gift of God, ignoring the biblical advice to be satisfied with these things, whether consciously or unconsciously, reflects a refusal to accept God's perspective on how to find satisfaction.

secrets of a satisfying life

Refusing to accept God's take on things can be a reflection of pride and a mind-set that says, "God may not be right on *this* subject. I know how to go about finding happiness." This faulty thinking does require repentance—a turning away from the incorrect perspective and the adoption of God's outlook. Without this action, your former outlook suggests that you're right and God is wrong.

What's stopping you from repenting and seeking God's forgiveness if you've realized you're in the wrong? Take a moment right now to ask God to cleanse your heart from the deceptive perspective that happiness cannot be found in the mundane things of this world. A few minutes in prayer will result in a changed perspective. This changed perspective will stimulate your pleasure in your job, home, church, and even your thoughts. Although nothing may change in these areas, *you* will change.

Follow Your Heart

Most people live in fear. They are afraid of what their family will say. Afraid of what their neighbors will think. They are even afraid of what their co-workers think—even though most of these colleagues play a minor role in their lives.

The newspaper counselor Ann Landers received an average of ten thousand letters each month, and nearly all of them were from people burdened with problems. She was asked if any one problem permeated the letters she received. She replied that the one problem above all others seemed to be fear. People were afraid of losing their health, their wealth, and their loved ones. People were afraid of life itself.[2]

In other words, people are afraid of living. Most people are afraid to follow their hearts because they fear criticism from their casual acquaintances or dear friends. According to Jesus, "where your treasure is, there your heart will be also" (Matt. 6:21). Hence one's treasure, or satisfaction, will always be found in close proximity to one's heart. The problem lies in mustering up the needed courage to follow your heart despite what others may say or think.

Following your heart is about following your dreams, passions, and emotional desires. As a Christian, I am aware that God gives me feelings, dreams, and the ability to sense and enjoy pleasure. We can draw again from Solomon's wisdom, as the Bible records him saying, "Be happy, young man, while you are young, and let your heart give you joy in the days of your youth. Follow the ways of your heart and whatever your eyes see, but know that for all these things God will bring you to judgment" (Eccles. 11:9). We are encouraged to follow our hearts, which will give us joy. This compliance to the heart is to start at an early age, not when we are retired and no longer care what others think. The younger we are, the more we should learn the habit that satisfaction is found in following our heart's passion. Playing it safe does not secure happiness!

Solomon qualifies his statement by concluding, "God will bring you to judgment." In other words, don't let your heart lead you to a destructive path that will be sure to bring God's judgment. All of us know someone who followed his or her heart down a path that led to personal or family destruction. This is not the type of journey Solomon is encouraging us to take. To avoid this destructive path, you should maintain a full commitment to the ethical and moral requirements of the Bible while pursuing your passions. At the same time, we human beings cannot allow fear to so grip our hearts that we become cowards to our passions because we are afraid that the temptation to do evil is lurking around the corner.

The Christian walk is a journey toward being conformed to the character and image of Christ. This walk assumes that we will take risks because we cannot maintain ongoing spiritual transformation without learning to overcome temptation.

In order to follow your heart, you cannot simply focus on avoiding temptation; rather, your focus should be on pursuing your desires. When your desires and passions are in line with the Holy Spirit's desires and the Bible's teaching, you should not hesitate to stay in hot pursuit of these precious dreams. Solomon's wise advice was "Be happy . . . and let your heart give you joy" (Eccles. 11:9). What is your heart saying to you? Or to put it another way, what would you do if you weren't afraid? In my book *Perfecting Your Purpose*, I walk readers through a forty-day journey to help them understand and fulfill their God-given purpose by being courageous.[3] Courage is the ability to pursue your life's passion in the face of various types of obstacles.

The Value of Courage

The importance or value of courage is not seen until courage surfaces during a crisis. An emperor besieged a town and would not listen to pleas for mercy. Finally he said he would let the women go, but they could only take with them what they could carry. The women came out of the houses with their husbands and children on their backs. When the emperor saw this, he cried, understanding at last the burden of courage. Similarly, if satisfaction is missing from your life, you must see this as a crisis. This view summons courage to the fore every time. Courage is the very ingredient that helps us conquer adversities and attain a life of satisfaction.

Courage asserts itself in many common ways: infants learn how to walk amidst all their falls and stumbles; physically challenged people complete marathons even if it takes several hours beyond the normal race time; single parents meet their children's needs on a daily basis; homemakers find meaningful lives outside of corporate America; and families decide to live complete lives after a severe family tragedy occurs. Every one of us must decide that our lives are worthy of joy. This joy is attained when you follow the desires of your heart as you walk the road of courage.

Go for It!

Let's return to the question, *What would you do if you weren't afraid?* Searching your heart will give you an accurate answer to this all-important question. Whatever your conclusion, you'll need to summon courage to realize that goal. Happy people adopt a reasonable threshold for personal happiness. That threshold is met when you make the decision to be happy, find enjoyment out of life, and follow your heart's desire. Go for it! Pursue a satisfying life!

4

the happy, hopeful perspective

When Kevin Johnson, a high school student, interviewed Ruth Sender, a Holocaust survivor, he asked, "What kept you alive during the Holocaust?" Her response came quickly:

Hope—hope was the reason to live through the camps. One of the things I remember about the Holocaust is that there was one woman who would perform a little ceremony to God in her bunk every night. There weren't candles or anything as they were all prohibited, but she used to say some prayers in her bunk. Because the bunks were three decks and if you lifted your head you would bump it against the bunk above you, maybe the opening was only a foot wide. But because we were so close, you could hear everything. But every night when she did this ceremony, everyone used to ridicule her and tell her that prayer was useless. But even that little ceremony gave us all some hope. So the hope came from everywhere.[1]

Some have said that perspective is reality. A positive mental view of your ideas, facts, historical experiences, and their interrelationships can create a happy and hopeful reality. Determining the sources of your feelings is a habit that creates a happy and hopeful perspective. According to research findings by two sociologists, Nerella Ramanaiah and Fred Detwiler, people who are least likely to overcome temporary disappointments are those who are unable to define the sources of their feelings.[2] If hope can saturate your thinking, your feelings are more apt to point you in the direction of developing a happy perspective toward life.

Oftentimes we are unhappy and we don't know why. We are unable to connect the dots and discover the reason for our gloomy outlook. Perhaps if we could determine the reason for our unhappy feelings, we could make a slight adjustment that would yield a more hopeful perspective on life. Unhappy people have the same experiences and range of life events as others. Happy people, however, observe the patterns in their thinking and make the necessary adjustments in order to yield pleasant feelings. These pleasant feelings surface from the hopeful perspective that is the anchor of happy people.

Years ago the *S-4* submarine was rammed by another ship and quickly sank just off the coast of Massachusetts. The entire crew was trapped in this prison house of death. Ships rushed to the scene of the disaster. We don't know what took place down in the sunken submarine, but we can be sure that the men clung bravely to life as the oxygen slowly gave out.

secrets of a satisfying life

A diver placed his helmeted ear to the side of the vessel and listened. He heard a tapping noise. Someone was tapping out a question in Morse Code. The question came slowly: "Is . . . there . . . any . . . hope?"

This seems to be the cry of humanity: "Is there any hope?" Hope, indeed, is the basis of all human existence! The need for hope was also summed up in this story told by the daily devotional booklet *Our Daily Bread*.

> While attending college, I visited a psychiatric institution with a group of students to observe various types of mental illness. The experience proved to be very disturbing. I remember one man who was called "No Hope Carter." His was a tragic case. A victim of venereal disease, he was going through the final stages when the brain is affected.
>
> Before he began to lose his mind, this man was told by the doctors that there was no known cure for him. He begged for one ray of light in his darkness, but had been told that the disease would run its inevitable course and end in death. Gradually his brain deteriorated and he became more and more despondent.
>
> When I saw him in his small, barred room about two weeks before he died, he was pacing up and down in mental agony. His eyes stared blankly, and his face was drawn and ashen. Over and over he muttered these two forlorn and fateful words: "No hope! No hope!" He said nothing else.[3]

Hopelessness is a coma of the soul. The comatose person—like "No Hope Carter"—falls into a prolonged state of spiritual unconsciousness. In the medical world, a comatose patient is unable to respond to his or her environment. Some call this condition being "brain dead." Drawing a parallel to the spiritual state of hopelessness, a person who has lost hope is unable to respond to new opportunities or prospects. They have experienced a spiritual brain death and have no expectations or thoughts of a better tomorrow. The absence of hope affects every dimension of this person's life, including their emotional, physical, psychological, and behavioral state.

When I began my counseling of Steve (not his real name), he had become so disillusioned from his wife's serial adultery that he fell into a state of hopelessness. Since Steve was a solid Christian, he chose to try to work out the marital problems through prayer and counseling. But because quick results were not on the horizon, he became spiritually comatose—he stopped caring about anything, even God's promises for his life. Despite a myriad of pastoral warnings, he also fell headlong into adultery in retaliation for his wife's unfaithfulness. As providence would have it, they both repented of their sins within days of one another. This couple took the road less traveled and rebuilt their marriage. I wish that all sad stories ended on such a happy note, but they don't—at least not in the real world. My contention, regardless of this fallen world, is that hopelessness should never be an option for pain management, even when sad stories don't end well.

Avoiding the Trap of Hopelessness

On a recent trip to Atlanta, I drove past a church on the outskirts of Stone Mountain, Georgia. The church was named Bridge of Hope. The tagline on the church's sign read: "The church where perfect people are prohibited." *What an unusual marketing strategy*, I thought. The church announced up front and boldly to the whole community that the prerequisite for entry is acknowledgment to yourself and to others, *beforehand*, that you are imperfect. The church's signage and beautiful name, Bridge of Hope, causes all passersby to conclude that hope is the antidote for imperfect people.

We live in an imperfect world, and we are imperfect people. That is, we are morally imperfect and prone to inconsistencies despite our greatest and most noble intentions. This human flaw is most likely the reason why the apostle Paul wrote concerning himself, "I do not understand what I do. For what I want to do I do not do, but what I hate I do" (Rom. 7:15). Despite our human frailty, God's love demonstrated through Christ's death on the cross was not based upon our good behavior. Christ died for us simply because he loved us. Although we were sinners—disconnected from God and disobedient to his laws—Christ died so that we might have eternal life. Love was extended for imperfect people in the same way hope is offered to imperfect people.

Navigating our way through the traps of pride, self-will, and an inflated ego is the way we escape hopelessness. These deadly psychological conditions usually cause us to think that we are perfect or that we are not in need of God's help. They fool us into thinking that we have the final word in the affairs of our lives. These traits keep us alienated from God by fostering a view that we can act independently of God and manage the outcomes of our lives. But true hope cannot be created when you consciously or unconsciously think that you are anything but imperfect and that you have no need for God in your life. These attitudes lead to a state of hopelessness.

Prayer, fasting, and even hanging around enthusiastic people serve as excellent weapons for combating hopelessness. You will quickly discover that enthusiasm is contagious. One Sunday morning during a period when I was down on myself, having fallen into the intellectual trap of overanalyzing my life and vision, God used a paraplegic named Joey to encourage me. Joey is about thirty years old and lives in a home run by the government for people with special needs. He began coming to my church several years ago. A van designed for chauffeuring people in wheelchairs pulled up to Christ Church one Sunday morning, and out came an attendant who wheeled Joey into the lobby of our cathedral. Since the pews in this historic building were not made to accommodate wheelchairs, the ushers wheeled Joey straight to the front of the church and stationed him in front of the first row of pews.

For the first few Sundays, I didn't really notice Joey because of the size of the congregation and the frequency of visitors. As time passed, however, I began to take note of Joey, whose wheelchair was faithfully positioned in front of the altar week after week. Our eyes connected a number of times as I preached. He would smile from ear to ear as he listened to the gospel message. Although he was physically unable to talk or to move his hands or feet, he would regularly request to come to our church, always wearing his infectious smile. Joey's disability also caused him to struggle to keep his head raised. Often his head would slump down and he would become completely oblivious to the world around him, sometimes even falling asleep after a long struggle to keep his head up.

That Sunday morning when I was feeling sorry for myself—thinking that my dreams and visions for the church were not happening as fast as I would like them to—I glanced in Joey's direction. Our eyes met, and the warmest smile broke out on his face. His smile communicated volumes to me. I thought that if he were able to speak, he would have given me the warmest hello anyone could give. If he were able to hug, I would have received the tightest squeeze of affection. And if he were able to shake hands, he would have given me the friendliest handshake of my life. Although Joey was physically unable to do any of these things, his smile melted my feelings of hopelessness. His smile gave me a fresh perspective: life was not so bad after all. I was reminded that I must fight against my feelings of hopelessness. And God used Joey—someone who clearly had more reasons than I did to feel a sense of hopelessness—to encourage me.

The Value of Hope

The Grand Ballroom of the Opryland Hotel in Nashville, Tennessee, was teeming with Christian leaders from every denomination in the United States. The February 2002 annual convention of the National Religious Broadcasters was to feature President George W. Bush as the honored guest speaker. I sat quietly with the throng of people who only dared to whisper to one another during this momentous event. We were eager to receive an encouraging message that would motivate us to continue serving the needs of the nation through Christian radio and television. President Bush started his speech with these words: "The government cannot give hope; only God can give us hope."

This introductory statement triggered a barrage of thoughts in my mind about the power of hope. I became preoccupied with these questions: What is hope? Whose is it to offer? How do we access it? What kind of power does it contain? The answers to these questions provide the fuel to help scores of people who have fallen into a state of hopelessness to fall in love with life once again.

Many types of power exist in the world, including electrical, mechanical, and fluid power. Electricity moves energy through cables, while mechanical power turns gears that drive engines. Water or other fluids can be used to create steam, heat, and other forms of energy. Society also uses various forms of power—including physical force, economic rewards or sanctions, ridicule, isolation, and even belief systems—in an attempt to control and influence people's actions. Apart from these external types of power, you will also find the internal spiritual power of hope, which Webster's dictionary defines as the ability to "expect or look forward to, with desire, and confidence."[4]

Hope Defined

Four common characteristics of hope will form the basis of our discussion throughout this chapter: (1) hope is vision for the future; (2) hope is promise; (3) hope creates an inner resolve; and (4) hope involves end time actions.

We will use these definitions to formulate a deeper understanding of the power of hope in helping us to achieve victory over life's most difficult circumstances. Hope is vitally important to every dimension of life, whether family, business, educational, or societal. Yet many people hold several inaccurate perceptions of what hope is.

Hope Is Not a Positive State of Mind

Hope is generally equated with an American overemphasis on positivism—the belief that all things will work out positively in the end. This obsession with positive attitude raises the question, according to Professor Barbara Held, "If there indeed now exists unprecedented pressure to accentuate the positive, could it then be that the pressure itself to be happy and optimistic contributes to at least some forms of unhappiness?"[5] This "tyranny of the positive attitude," writes Held, is influencing Americans into thinking that a positive state of mind is "necessary for (a sense of) well-being."[6]

This positive state of mind is misleading in view of the true meaning of hope. Hope at its core is never destructive, nor does it lead to an obsession. I am not suggesting that we should not be positive or that we should have a negative outlook on life. I am simply saying that hope cannot be equated with a positive mind-set. They are two entirely different things.

Hope Is Not Passive Optimism

Another incorrect, though popular, perspective is one that equates hope with passive optimism. In a nonchalant style, hope is presented this way: *If it turns out positively, it was meant to be anyway.* This concept of hope raises the question of whether passive optimism has a place in the emotional, psychological, or physical world. Nonetheless, it is viewed as the "right" attitude to have since being optimistic is considered to be far better than holding a negative view. This optimistic definition of hope is the politically correct meaning used in the marketplace today. The problem is that positive thinking offers no real power to cause change. This definition of hope is limiting and incorrect.

I am thrilled, however, that the real meaning of hope is far more comprehensive, accurate, and befitting. Hope has a greater place in society and in your life than simply thinking positively or being passively optimistic.

The True Meaning of Hope

The true meaning of hope is the one God assigns. God's hope, as proclaimed throughout the Bible, is like no other hope that exists. According to the Scriptures, hope unites God with the one hoping. Paul writes, "May the God of hope fill you with all joy and peace as you trust in him, so that you may overflow with hope by the power of the Holy Spirit" (Rom. 15:13). Not only does God offer hope, he is called the God of hope. Greek scholar Everett Harrison indicates that the expression *the God of hope* means "the God who inspires hope and imparts it to his children. He can be counted on to fulfill what yet remains to be accomplished for them."[7]

God's definition of hope involves his person. He is connected with his people, and his power is always available through this hope connection. Hope forges a partnership between God and the person hoping. This alliance brings God into the emotional, physical, intellectual, and spiritual equation. Hope can release power to the believer who is facing all kinds of seemingly impossible circumstances. Biblical hope is about embracing future and eternal promises. Although these promises may appear distant to us, they were earned by Christ two thousand years ago. His death, burial, and resurrection sealed every one of those innumerable promises.

The great love story of hope is simply this: God says, "Give me your sins and I will give you the hope of glory—my Son." It is not an even trade, yet it is what God wants. We exchange our sins for a place in heaven through Christ's redemptive love.

In Christ, when we hope, we have a connection to God and his power. This hope connection binds God to his children's present and future actions so that our future is intact. The four definitions of hope mentioned earlier also form the basis for seeing the power of hope: (1) hope is vision for the future; (2) hope is promise; (3) hope creates an inner resolve; and (4) hope involves end time actions.

1. Hope Is Vision for the Future

The word *vision* means *a realistic, credible, attractive future state*. When you have hope, you have vision for tomorrow. Hopeful people honestly believe that tomorrow is going to be better than today. Paul writes: "But hope that is seen is no hope at all. Who hopes for what he already has? But if we hope for what we do not yet have, we wait for it patiently" (Rom. 8:24–25). One meaning of hope is having a vision for the future—believing something will materialize in the future that you don't have today. This definition of hope is not only found within the biblical narrative. Behavioral scientists—people who study human actions and reactions—have defined hope to mean "a sense of reach that inspires and motivates."[8]

Abraham possessed vision for the future. Through the power of hope he was able to wait patiently until the future revealed him as the father of many nations (see Rom. 4:18). Although Abraham's life was saddled with all kinds of challenges—including fighting against doubt and unbelief and fathering a child outside of his marriage to Sarah—hope empowered him to recognize that his life was not going to end without embracing his dreams of the future. When hope is seen as vision, ideas begin to surface that jump-start the future, calling forth the skills, talents, and resources required to achieve that future state.

People who possess a compelling vision have not given up on life. Hope shines through their vision, communicating that the condition of their soul is good. If a psychologist examines a person who has suffered a tragedy and finds that the person shows a healthy psychological outlook, the doctor must conclude that the person is emotionally healthy. Such is the case when vision is evident—the soul is healthy because hope is present.

2. Hope Is Promise

Hope provides the soul a perspective that exclaims, "God's promises await me. Life is not over; everything will be okay!" Promises are precious plans, goals, and objectives that God has outlined for each of us. Imagine one of the darkest periods in the life of the nation of Israel. The prophet Jeremiah sent a letter to the surviving elders who were among the exiles in Babylon following Israel's defeat to this dreaded enemy. The exiles were severely crippled emotionally. They were slaves to the Babylonians, and they saw no sign they would ever be released. Jeremiah's letter conveyed a prophetic word—a message from God—that said: "'For I know the plans I have for you,' declares the LORD, 'plans to prosper you and not to harm you, plans to give you hope and a future'" (Jer. 29:11). Can you imagine how the exiled Jews must have felt when reading about how God had not disowned them? The letter reassured them that he still had promises awaiting them, packaged in the form of hope. When your life seems to be falling apart and the future appears dim, that is the perfect time to revisit the Bible to rediscover God's promises.

One of the most famous Christian classics is *Pilgrim's Progress*. This allegory, written by John Bunyan, contains several characters we can readily identify with because of their fears, their challenges, and how they stumbled upon solutions that kept them motivated in their search for the celestial city—a metaphor for God's salvation. A conversation between two of the characters, Christian and Hopeful, helps explain how hope can be defined as promise:

> Now a little before it was day, good Christian, as one half-amazed, broke out in passionate speech, "What a fool am I thus to lie in a stinking Dungeon, when I may as well be at liberty. I have a Key in my bosom called Promise that will,

I am persuaded, open any lock in Doubting Castle." Then said Hopeful, "That's good news. Good Brother, pluck it out of thy bosom and try." And the prison gates flew open.[9]

The key called Promise unlocked the dungeon doors for Christian and Hopeful, and it will unlock your prison of hopelessness and despair.

God does not abandon us when we're feeling disillusioned by life's painful moments. His promises stand as a beacon of hope, calling us to emerge out of all kinds of painful circumstances. God makes an eternal commitment to help us. Isaiah 43:1 states that it was God who created you, it was God who formed you, it was God who redeemed you, and it is God who calls you by name. God's prophetic word to you is: "You are mine." Sometimes when we go through hard times, we are tempted to think, *My life will never amount to anything. I don't see anything better on the horizon.* Remember, God said, "You are mine. You belong to me."

Each football season the Texas Longhorns play the Oklahoma Sooners in the "neutral" city of Dallas. Thousands of fans from each team invade the city to witness the clash between these two arch rivals. Sometimes the conflict extends beyond the playing field. One year a scuffle broke out in the stands and a handful of men were arrested, taken to jail, and forced to pay $250 bail. One fan didn't have bail money. All he had was his driver's license and his Neiman Marcus credit card. He showed it to the judge, who said, "You can't pay bail with that. You're spending the weekend in jail." The man used his one phone call to call the Neiman Marcus store and tell them his story. The request made its way up the company ladder until finally a vice president said, "This man is one of our customers; we'll help him out." They paid his bail and charged it to his account.[10]

God's loyalty to you is even greater than the loyalty this retailer has for its customers. I'm not saying this story is a perfect parallel to your spiritual life, but it illustrates the point. You belong to him, and when things get out of control, remember that he doesn't turn his back on you or withdraw his promises. They still stand wrapped in hope. Hope is defined as promise.

3. Hope Creates an Inner Resolve

"Time heals the brokenhearted." In most cases, I would tend to agree with this cliché. Emotional and psychological wounds most often heal over time. A marriage ravaged by adultery or repeated actions that cause distrust can be healed over time. The challenge most people face when confronting this kind of problem is that the pain is so traumatic that they react in a final way without looking for hope. When hope is not grasped, pain drives your actions and decisions. This style of pain management is one of the worst ways to seek healing or to resolve conflict. If you take a step back from the pressure of the circumstances, you will see hope as an inner resolve that heals the pain by pointing to a possibility of future pleasure, joy, trust, and wholeness.

The psalmist encourages himself with these words: "Why are you downcast, O my soul? Why so disturbed within me? Put your hope in God, for I will yet praise him, my Savior and my God" (Ps. 42:5–6). Although written as a song thousands of years ago, these words are offered to us today as the perspective we should have on hope. Hope creates an inner resolve to deal with conflict and pain.

The sons of a priest named Korah wrote Psalm 42 to remind the Jewish community, "When you are disturbed within, put your hope in God." In other words, since hope entails the future, some conflicts can only be resolved through hope, or over time. If you are looking for instantaneous healing, you probably won't find it. That is why so many people make rash decisions only to later discover that their pain drove them into making those poor choices.

Professor of psychology Dr. E. Mavis Hetherington did a forty-year study on the impact of divorce; in it she discovered a fantastic fact about one group that was able to fully resolve the emotional pain. She called this group the Enhancers; these people represent only 20 percent of the divorced community. Hetherington wrote, "Successful at work, Enhancers also succeed socially, as parents, and often in new marriages."[11] Their success was attributed to the fact that they did not allow the failure of divorce to define them but allowed the power of hope to bring an inner resolve to facing the past relational conflict. As you can see, scientific findings validate biblical reality. If you simply give hope a chance, you will discover that the power of hope will create an inner resolve to face your pain.

4. Hope Involves End Time Actions

The theological word *eschatology* is a fancy way of referring to the study of end times. Hope must also be viewed in eschatological terms—in light of eternity and not simply focusing on next week, next month, or next year. Biblical hope exists when we focus on God's eternal plans. Paul makes this clear in the opening remarks of his letter to Titus, where he writes: "Paul, a servant of God and an apostle of Jesus Christ for the faith of God's elect and the knowledge of the truth that leads to godliness—a faith and knowledge resting on the hope of eternal life, which God, who does not lie, promised before the beginning of time" (Titus 1:1–2).

Hope's full meaning extends beyond this world and into the one that is to come. To have hope *today* for eternal life *tomorrow* means that you understand the value of planning with an end-times perspective in mind.

My wife, Marlinda, and I recognize that part of our spiritual legacy to be passed on to our children is their ability to handle money. So we ratcheted up our training on money management during their preteen years. At first they resisted the idea of budgeting—planning how their money was going to be spent and saved—because they saw it as restrictive. But after many conversations about the value of money and their need to prove themselves as good stewards to God, they finally embraced it.

Our conviction was that we wanted God to be able to trust our children with money as they grew to adulthood. Over the course of our working lives, we all manage large sums of money, so we believe teaching our children the importance of handling money according to God's principles is important. The consequences of mismanaging money due to shortsightedness can be staggering. Most people never think about their future, though it is certain.

The Office of Consumer Affairs reported in 1997 that the use of general purpose credit cards jumped from 56 percent of all families in 1989 to about 66 percent in 1995. About 52 percent always paid off their balances, 20 percent paid off sometimes, and 28 percent hardly ever paid them off. This lax attitude toward debt elimination further entrenches the baby boomer into a financial hole.[12] Saving and managing money is utilizing the same attitude behind the meaning of hope: hope is about achieving end-time rewards from actions taken today.

A man living in Southern California was on his way to work one morning in his brand new BMW. Suddenly, the big one hit: the earth began to tremble under his wheels, and the car was swallowed by the earth. The man was seriously

secrets of a satisfying life

injured, but as he climbed out of the wreckage, he didn't even notice that his left arm had been cut off at the elbow. He just stood by the side of the road, viewing the wreckage and crying out, "Oh no, my Beemer, my Beemer!" A man who had witnessed the disaster said to him, "How can you be crying about your car? Don't you realize that your arm has been cut off?" The man looked down in horror at his missing limb and said, "Oh no! My Rolex! My Rolex!"

If your heart is consumed by the things of this world, you will never see the value of having an eternal hope. Sometimes the only way the present complexities make sense is when they are interpreted in light of the eternal definition of hope. Ask yourself this question: Is my problem really all that bad, in light of an eternity with God? The answer for every child of God is a resounding no! This is what Paul was laboring for the Christians at Corinth to understand when he wrote, "If only for this life we have hope in Christ, we are to be pitied more than all men" (1 Cor. 15:19). The apostle was informing us that our sights and values should be ultimately placed in eternal things and not temporal ones.

As you embrace the habit of living with a hopeful perspective, you will find yourself enjoying one of the secrets to living a satisfying life.

5

living your dreams

On a recent airplane trip, I sat next to a lady who was quite talkative. We went back and forth about our lives until finally she popped the question that most pastors dread. "So, what do you do?"

"I am a life management specialist," I replied.

"What's that?" she asked.

"I help people straighten out their lives. I show them how to manage their lives at a more rewarding level."

"How do you do that?" she asked.

"I simply help people discover their life purpose and build their lives on that foundation. Included with that perspective, I point people to the author of their purpose—God. I also help them put values in place that guide the way they relate to their purpose, God, family, and the world around them."

If you're thinking, *Pastor David Ireland, you* lied *to that lady*—no, I did not! Isn't being a *pastor* synonymous with being a *life management specialist?* My euphemism allowed me to give this dear lady a free lesson about getting her life in order.

Discovering your purpose is foundational to achieving satisfaction in life. Coming to grips with who you are, who you are not, and what you were created to be is essential to understanding your purpose in life. Each one of us has a destiny which serves as a catalyst to our actions and behavior. After thirty-three years of practicing law, Raymond Noble, former Deputy Attorney General of the state of New Jersey, made a radical decision to return to his childhood dream and become a Franciscan friar. He had made a decision to become a priest at the age of fourteen, but when he experienced a terrible auto accident en route to seminary, Noble decided that it was a sign the priesthood wasn't for him.[1] However, like so many others, Noble found happiness by reconnecting with his destiny.

Identifying Your Purpose

Identifying your purpose is often like looking for your car keys or reading glasses. You turn the house upside down searching for the darn thing, and there it is—right under your nose. In 1917 a young Bible student named Cameron Townsend could not afford to pay tuition, so he signed a one-year contract with a publishing company that sold Spanish Bibles in Central America. Since the pay was good, he reasoned that in a year he would be able to resume his education. Townsend soon discovered a problem. Six out of ten Guatemalans spoke only Cakchiquel (Koch-i-kell), an Indian language, and could not read at all. So they had little interest in his Bibles.

Townsend realized that he had no answer when one of the natives asked, "Why doesn't your God speak my language?" He decided to stay in Central America and learn Cakchiquel, even though the language had never been written. Despite the fact that Townsend was not a linguist—or even a college graduate—he devised an alphabet and put the language into writing. After twelve years of hard work, Townsend presented the first book ever published in Cakchiquel to the president of Guatemala. The book was the New Testament. During this time Townsend had also founded five schools, a clinic, a print shop, and an orphanage. This was only the beginning of the achievements of this great man of God. Temporary financial problems led Cameron Townsend to a life's work that changed the course of Central American history.[2]

Townsend's purpose of being a Bible translator was right under his nose. What would have happened if he hadn't tried to solve the problem of the language barrier that he was facing? I would wager a guess: he would have probably earned the needed tuition to re-enroll in Bible College, graduated, and searched high and low for his purpose. Thankfully, he was astute. He recognized that right under his nose was an opportunity to help people learn about God in their own language. As in a relatively high number of cases, the opportunity right under Townsend's nose was God's purpose for his life.

Distractions from our past often keep us from moving toward the discovery of our life's purpose. Purpose deals with the future, not the past. If you are living in the past but are unaware of it, your eyes must be opened to its deceptive nature. People who live in the past tend to do three things almost habitually: (1) they seek to get even with those who have hurt them; (2) they have a nostalgic view of the past;

and (3) they consider themselves too irrevocably damaged to pursue their purpose and destiny. Let's explore the problems associated with each of these perspectives.

Seeking to Get Even

Seeking to get even indicates that you are living in the past. This warped sense of justice may also provoke dwellers of the past to seek revenge by outdoing what their victimizer has achieved in their life. Being aware of God's justice, you should instead seek the peace that comes from the Scripture that encourages:

> Do not repay anyone evil for evil. Be careful to do what is right in the eyes of everybody. If it is possible, as far as it depends on you, live at peace with everyone. Do not take revenge, my friends, but leave room for God's wrath, for it is written: "It is mine to avenge; I will repay," says the Lord.
>
> Romans 12:17–19

Being in the position of second-in-command of the most powerful nation of the world, Joseph could have behaved horribly, especially during times of national and international famine. He was the doorkeeper to the nation's surplus food. Anyone inside or outside the nation who wanted to purchase food had to pass through Joseph (see Gen. 41:56–57). Had he not let go of his past, he could have abused his position by having penniless women pay for food for their families using sexual favors. He could have also found a painful way to get even with Potiphar and his lying wife for the years he spent behind bars on trumped-up charges of attempted rape. He did nothing of the sort. Rather, Joseph understood that vengeance was God's to dole out, not his. Forgiveness had been worked in his heart.

Joseph's purity of heart demonstrated a powerful victory over his painful past (see Genesis 36–50). His victimization began when his jealous brothers sold him into slavery. To cover their horrible behavior, they soaked his coat in a pool of blood and told their father, Jacob, that a wild beast had devoured Joseph. Joseph's trials did not stop there. He was sold to Potiphar, an Egyptian leader, by the group who bought Joseph from his wicked brothers. To top off Joseph's pain, he was later imprisoned for the false charges of attempted rape levied against him by Potiphar's wife. She did this because he would not stoop to the level of having an affair with her. So when Joseph let go of his past by forgiving all of his victimizers, he really forgave. Forgiveness is a wonderful gift that you must regularly thank God for by applying it to the broken areas of your life.

Holding a Nostalgic View

The past plays like a broken record in the mind. A nostalgic view reflects a homesick perspective, one that wistfully yearns for a return to something in the past. Such a viewpoint causes you to constantly live with a perspective that deceives you into thinking that the past really wasn't all that bad. This victim of the past does not seek to apply the "50/20 principle" (of Gen. 50:20) the way that Joseph did in saying, "You intended to harm me, but God intended it for good." Instead, this person maintains a nostalgic view of yesterday.

Joseph was not trapped in the past by a nostalgic view. He recognized that the painful events in his life had, in fact, happened and that they had hurt. But freedom from the past came as he opened the door of forgiveness.

Thinking That You Are Irrevocably Damaged

The human spirit is resilient. It bounces back from death's door. Like the Energizer Bunny of the battery commercials, we keep going and going and going. Joseph sprung from the pit to the prison and into the palace. He did not succumb to the notion that his trials had irrevocably damaged him. He was still alive. He still wanted to live. He still had a purpose.

Some of the world's greatest men and women have been saddled with disabilities and painful adversities, yet they did not give in to the thought that they had been irrevocably damaged. Cripple him, and you have a Sir Walter Scott. Lock him in a prison cell, and you have a John Bunyan. Bury him in the snows of Valley Forge, and you have a George Washington. Raise him in abject poverty, and you have an Abraham Lincoln. Subject him to bitter religious prejudice, and you have a Benjamin Disraeli. Strike him down with infantile paralysis, and he becomes a Franklin D. Roosevelt.[3] The list of people who rejected the rejection of this world is endless. Their testimonies cheer us on to overcome our own hurdles.

Del Elkind, who works with disabled students in Peterborough, New Hampshire, asked *Dilbert* creator Scott Adams to advise a boy who wanted to become a cartoonist. "Most success springs from an obstacle or failure," Adams wrote. "I became a cartoonist largely because I failed in my goal of becoming a successful executive. One of my favorite cartoonists is John Callahan, a quadriplegic. He recognized he was uniquely able to make cartoons about physically disadvantaged people and nobody would criticize him. I recommend that your student reflect on the things that bother him most. What ticks him off? That's where his cartooning fuel will be found."[4]

Thinking that you are irrevocably damaged because of disabilities or roadblocks need not hamper you from achieving your life's purpose. Resiliency is in the genes of human beings. All you need to do now is discover your life's purpose, which may be right under your nose.

Look Under Your Nose!

In order to see the gold mine of your purpose, which may be lying right under your nose, you must take three action steps. You must be willing to (1) step back, (2) step out, and (3) step in.

1. Step Back

Taking a step back means becoming intentional about disentangling yourself from your day-to-day hurriedness, emotions, and behaviors in order to gain a clearer perspective of life. We sometimes use the word *retreat* to describe the process of stepping back from a crisis or a hectic pace to gain the clarity needed to redirect our lives. Jesus taught his disciples how to step back from the constant pressure of their ministry responsibilities so that their lives were driven by purpose and not by people's demands or opinions or by their own need to be wanted by others.

Taking a step back is especially important following great victories or great failures. In the following account taken from the Gospel of Mark, we learn that the twelve apostles were instructed to take a step back following a time of significant accomplishment in their teaching and evangelism efforts.

The apostles gathered around Jesus and reported to him all they had done and taught. Then, because so many people were coming and going that they did not even have a chance to eat, he said to them, "Come with me by yourselves to a quiet place and get some rest." So they went away by themselves in a boat to a solitary place.

Mark 6:30–32

Jesus's words "Come with me by yourselves to a quiet place and get some rest" (v. 31) provided four levels of instruction to the apostles under the overarching theme of stepping back. First, the apostles were to step back *with* Jesus. Simply going on a retreat or sitting by the beach staring out at the ocean's waves is not good enough. You must take Jesus *with you* on the retreat. You must include God in the equation in order to step back effectively. Your purpose cannot be discovered apart from the One who created purpose and created you.

Second, we learn that Jesus told the disciples to "come with me *by yourselves.*" The therapeutic power of solitude is enormous. Solitude with God is to you what water is to flowers. Without water flowers wilt, wither, and eventually die. However, the opposite is wonderful to witness. As soon as the water hits the roots of the flowers, they grow and radiate the mystery of God's beauty through the energy they have absorbed. Likewise, when you step back to be alone with God, you draw strength and life sustenance from the dynamic spiritual interchange. The result is that your life, which may have been wilting away due to lack of purpose, begins to revive as you discover who you were created to be.

Third, Jesus's counsel called for a stepping back to a *quiet place.* The quiet place is where you get to know yourself and discover your inclinations. Become intentional about stepping back and getting alone with God. Turn off the CD player, the television, and the radio. Shut off the computer, fax machine, and cell phone. Block out as much of life's artificial noises as possible so that you may hear God's voice whisper to your soul the purpose for which he has created you.

Fourth, Jesus's instruction, "Come with me by yourselves to a quiet place and get some rest," helps us to see that rest is essential to becoming effective. The word *rest* in the original Greek—the language in which the New Testament was penned—means *inner rest* or *to be at peace*. Jesus was telling the apostles, "Guys, if you want to walk effectively in your purpose, learn to intentionally step back and get some inner rest from the pressures of life."

Time to step back in order to regroup and recharge was necessary to bring the apostles' lives back into balance. We can easily tell that they faced an imbalance, since they did not even have a chance to eat! If you are not eating, sleeping, effectively handling your basic responsibilities, or giving significant attention to your God-given purpose, your life is out of balance. The task of attending to your purpose cannot be overlooked since God created all of us with a specific purpose in mind. If you are unclear about your purpose, this is even more reason to step back and reassess what you're doing and where you're going with your life. In so doing, you will come away with a clear direction regarding God's purpose for you on the earth. Why not consider taking a step back the way Jesus prescribed? You will be enormously benefited by the experience, and you will also draw closer to the Lord.

Do you remember the last time you stepped back from life's hectic pace? What did you discover? Try to build on that discovery of your calling and assignment so that your next period of stepping back will bring you even closer to your life's purpose.

2. Step Out

In another Bible passage, Jesus demonstrates that after you step back, you must step out.

> One of those days Jesus went out to a mountainside to pray, and spent the night praying to God. When morning came, he called his disciples to him and chose twelve of them, whom he also designated apostles.
>
> Luke 6:12–13

Again we see Jesus intentionally taking some time alone to recharge and get a fresh perspective about where his life is headed and what his next significant objective should be. In this passage, the need to designate some of his followers as apostles—people commissioned for a definite purpose—was important to him. After stepping back to pray, reflect, and gain the power of introspection, Jesus made the decision to take action or to step out.

After you step back, you must step out. Stepping *back* is reflective and introspective, while stepping *out* involves action—the acting out of the wisdom gained during the period of solitude. Stepping *out* indicates that the needed decisions have been made. This directional step provides the momentum for outward changes in your behavior and lifestyle. The act of stepping out shows that you have received answers to your mental, spiritual, and emotional questions about your life's purpose. And even if you don't know your exact plan of action, your conclusion is sure: "I am going to begin a life of purposefulness. I am going to do something about my situation!"

George Cameron makes this kind of declaration daily. Cameron is alive today due to the kidney donation of Clay Jones, a high school football player in Texas who died as a result of being struck by lightning. Although Cameron doesn't know the answer to his life's purpose yet, he wholeheartedly believes that God must have some purpose for his still being alive. Feelings of heightened spirituality are almost universal among organ recipients, according to Lisa Kory, executive director of the Transplant Recipients International Organization. She says, "They are so filled with awe and inspiration . . . they want to be a better father, brother, sister, and worker." Cameron said that before receiving the transplanted kidney, a lot of his life was spent in careless living: "I gambled, I drank to excess, I didn't take care of myself." But knowing that he carries the kidney of such a blameless young man has affected him greatly. He now works harder at being patient and loving and respectful of life and other people.[5]

Cameron's decision to *step out* of a self-destructive pattern came as a result of a life experience. On the other hand, Jesus intentionally stepped back so that he could come up with a plan that could be implemented by the natural sequence of stepping out. While in prayer he arrived at the decision to ordain twelve apostles. Reaching a conclusion leads to stepping out.

After thinking deeply about my weight problem and talking about it with others, I finally made the decision to step out and do something about it. I set a weight loss goal of twenty-five pounds over a period of three months. I hired a professional trainer for a series of three training sessions per week over the twelve-week period. By the eighth week, I had lost twenty pounds because, according to my trainer, I had a "passion reason." This phrase captures the essence of what drove me to lose the next five pounds in four more weeks. This victory stemmed from my stepping out and passionately pursuing what was clearly an aspect of God's plan for my life.

Don't focus on what triggers the need to step out. Stepping out is the issue. Make the decision to step out and then do it!

3. Step In

After you step *back*, you must step *out*, and then you should step *in*. Stepping *in* speaks of implementing the decisions reached in the stepping *out* phase. Drawing again from Luke 6:12–13, Jesus demonstrates that after he reached the conclusion in prayer to ordain twelve apostles, he had to actually execute the decisions thereafter. What good is taking a step back to recharge and formulate a new plan if you are not going to take a step in and implement the decisions you've made?

After several years as a senior engineer with a civil engineering firm, I became confused about my life's purpose. Engineering was no longer fulfilling, even though I was quite young—then only in my mid-twenties. My wife and I had started a new church plant that had now grown to thirty people. By this time my bi-vocational status was wearing on me mentally. I found myself becoming more passionate about the ministry, even though the church was struggling and quite young. I decided to shut myself away for a few days to get God's perspective about my life. These questions were gnawing at me: Where do I belong? What is my purpose at this juncture of my life? Am I to remain in engineering or enter into full-time ministry as a vocation? Since God was the only one who could answer those questions, I decided to "go up to the mountain" and seek his face for clear directions. I was taking a step back to hear God's wisdom on the matter.

Since I did not have the extra funds to go away for a three-day retreat in the Pocono Mountains, I decided to go into our spare bedroom and seek God. I told my wife, Marlinda, that I wasn't to be disturbed because I would be seeking God for the next three days. I scheduled the appropriate time off from my job and prepared myself to fast and pray during those three days. Armed with a Bible, a notepad, and a pen, I retreated to the guest bedroom to be shut away with God. At the end of three days, I had no doubt in my mind that God wanted me to dedicate my life to full-time ministry. I was crystal clear on this fact. After the shut-in time, I shared the decision with Marlinda, and she wholeheartedly agreed.

Although I had stepped back and reflected on my situation, I had not yet stepped in. My tiny congregation could not afford to financially support me and my family—a wife and a one-year-old daughter—especially with a salary equal to an engineer's. So I decided to take a half-step. I made a proposal to my boss about working part time, just two days each week. He agreed. I did this for about two months before I felt the internal pressure resurfacing. Yet I was afraid to "step in" to the realm of trusting God regarding his purpose for my life. Marlinda and I discussed the issue once again. She agreed that full-time ministry was part of God's purpose for our lives. So we decided to use our faith by *stepping in* to God's complete plan. The following week I resigned from my engineering position. Remarkably, the church grew to double the number of members within six weeks. Because I stepped in to God's plan, he matched my salary, and we have not looked back since. That was some eighteen years ago, and I have learned that Jesus's advice to step back, step out, and step in is key to discovering your life's purpose.

Where are you in all of this? Better yet, where are you in proximity to embracing your dreams, your goals, and your life's purpose? God has placed you here on earth for a purpose. Therefore, a satisfied life cannot be attained apart from the pursuit and fulfillment of your purpose.

6

happiness and busyness: strange bedfellows

I have always heard it said, "If you want something done, give it to a busy person." I have discovered an even better idea: if you want something done, give it to a happy person.

Happy people are usually busy people who have learned to build periods of rest and relaxation into their busy schedules. Most people who live beyond sixty years, regardless of culture, ethnicity, or national origin, have come to realize that an excessively busy lifestyle erodes away happiness. They seem to have given themselves permission to live their lives in rebellion to society. While most people are frantically working, hurrying, and worrying in an effort to improve the quality and happiness of their lives, you generally find senior citizens going for leisurely walks, taking meaningless excursions, and even enjoying sightseeing drives in their own neighborhoods.

What have these older folks discovered that the rest of us have missed? At face value, it seems like a key to happiness is being over sixty. But a deeper look reveals that happiness is linked to your goals and your outlook on life. The 1996 study indicates one has a 43 percent greater probability of achieving satisfaction with life when one's goals are connected with one's philosophy of life.[1] In other words, if in your philosophy rest and relaxation are important goals, the probability of achieving your goal with a happy state of mind increases by 43 percent simply because you institute periods of rest and relaxation. The elderly have unknowingly stumbled on this finding. The habit of integrating busyness with relaxation is easy to understand but not necessarily easy to do. You don't have to be old, but you do have to give yourself permission to rebel against a lot of cultural assumptions. One such assumption is that the busier you are, the faster you'll achieve happiness.

Don't confuse taking needed rests with laziness—which is a time-waster that has no inherent benefit. As you weave rest times into your busyness, evaluate whether these breathers are being used appropriately or are simply a mask for laziness.

Once a man was so lazy that he actually won $100,000 in cash in a contest for being the laziest man in the world. The contest, sponsored by a millionaire, ended after a three-month search to find the laziest man in the world. The winner was found on a beach with his skin peeling and burning from the noonday sun.

"Why are you laying on the beach in the scorching sun?" the millionaire asked the lazy man.

"When I came out here the sun was not up, and I'm not moving," he replied.

"Here's your money," the millionaire said.

"Roll me over and put it in my pocket," replied the lazy man.

Taking periodic rests may seem unproductive, maybe even a little boring. However, rest enables you to maintain a fresh charge as you pursue your dreams. As simple as this principle may seem, many people have a hard time applying it to their lives. You may need a paradigm shift in your thinking in order to appreciate this integrated approach. Work needs to be interspersed with relaxation in order to enjoy the job and achieve satisfaction in life. It's like the story about Sam, who had to be persuaded to do something that would ultimately benefit him.

Everybody but Sam had signed up for a new company pension plan that called for a small employee contribution. The company was paying the rest. Unfortunately, 100 percent employee participation was needed for the plan to be adopted. Sam's boss and his fellow workers pleaded with him, but to no avail. In Sam's opinion, the plan would never pay off. Finally the company president called Sam into his office. "Sam," he said, "here's a copy of the new pension plan, and here's a pen. I want you to sign the papers. I'm sorry, but if you don't sign, you're fired as of right now." Sam signed the papers immediately. "Now," said the president, "would you mind telling me why you couldn't have signed earlier?"

"Well, sir," replied Sam, "nobody explained it to me so clearly before."

Some people need the principle of integrating work and relaxation explained to them in much the same way. "You have to rest," the doctor says, "or you will be dead in one year." This confrontational manner is the only language some people understand.

Happy people are busy people who have developed the habit of integrating rest into their fast-paced schedules. Regular rests can provide four steps to a busy person trying to figure out how to be happy at the same time: (1) take regular rests, (2) learn how to recharge, (3) develop your personal work style, and (4) enjoy the process.

Take Regular Rests

One man challenged another to an all-day wood chopping contest. The challenger worked very hard, stopping only for a brief lunch break. The other man had a leisurely lunch and took several breaks during the day. At the end of the day, the challenger was surprised and annoyed to find that the other fellow had chopped substantially more wood than he had. "I don't get it," he said. "Every time I checked, you were taking a rest, yet you chopped more wood than I did."

"But you didn't notice," said the winning woodsman, "that when I sat down to rest, I was sharpening my ax."

Times of relaxation should be viewed as recharging episodes, not wasted time. The defeated woodsman worked harder but not necessarily smarter or more productively. He viewed rest times as interruptions rather than as opportunities to recharge his energy level. The winning woodsman viewed rest periods as times for sharpening his ax and reviving his energy level.

While I am not promoting being lazy or living boring lives, I am suggesting that excessive busyness for the sake of pursuing happiness is also not a good idea to adopt. Excessive busyness does not produce happiness any more than excessive laziness. The habit of integrating hard work with regular rest periods is the discipline you should seek to embrace. How many times have you heard a grandmotherly or grandfatherly type say, "I wish I had spent more time with my children when they were little, rather than working so many hours at the office." This statement has almost become a cliché, yet younger generations are not catching on. Why wait until you're over sixty years old for this truth about happiness to register? Hear it now and adopt it as a lifestyle principle.

Talk with a person over sixty and you will quickly learn that behind every wrinkled face is a story. The one question you should ask that will help you glean from their experiences is this: If you had to live your life over again, what would you do differently in order to be happy? Almost invariably you will hear them say, "I would slow down and build in more opportunities for rest and relaxation." The problem is not busyness but *excessive busyness*, the kind that compels people to work constantly in the hope of realizing their dream. It may be a dream house, a dream car, or some other prize that they simply cannot live without. People sacrifice everything, even common sense, to attain these things. The problem is that the zeal that motivates them to work so hard leaves them unfulfilled when the goal is attained or consumed with bitterness if it is not achieved.

Periods of rest and refreshing must be built into your life so that you can attain happiness along the way toward achieving your dreams. Unfortunately, most people work their fingers to the bone in the hope of attaining happiness at the end of their life when all their dreams are realized. This approach seldom works. The majority of people who have chosen this route live out their latter years in a state of frustration and regret.

Each of us is given 168 hours in a week. Most people distribute these hours as follows: 8 hours a day for sleep, 3 hours a day for food, and 10 hours a day (5 days per week) for work and travel. This leaves approximately 35–40 hours each week unaccounted for. Not surprisingly, studies show that most American families watch television 35–45 hours per week.

While I am not suggesting that television watching is off limits, I am asserting that television watching alone does not provide the necessary reenergizing that your body, soul, and mind need. What should you do? The Bible shares this insightful advice: "So watch your step. Use your head. Make the most of every chance you get. These are desperate times! Don't live carelessly, unthinkingly. Make sure you understand what the Master wants" (Eph. 5:15–17 Message). Heeding this advice by making the most of every opportunity—by using your rest times in ways that truly recharge you—will result in greater overall fulfillment.

Learn How to Recharge

In a 1998 study of college students, researchers concluded that those students carrying a more demanding schedule had a 15 percent higher satisfaction with life.[2] This shows that busyness that does not adversely affect one's stress level can contribute to happiness. What gives *you* rest may not be what brings *me* rest and vice versa. In my case, during restful times you will find me either jogging, writing, engaged in a meaningful intellectual discussion, or curled up on the sofa with a good book. I have learned that my mind must be at least mildly stimulated for rest to occur.

My wife, on the other hand, recharges by spending time alone. In the early days of our marriage I viewed her private moments as rejection or possible disappointment with me. The first time I watched Marlinda walk into the bedroom and dim the lights, I was perplexed. It was too early for bed, yet she seemed to be shutting down for the night. Had I offended her? Why was she in the bedroom sitting in silence? I had to go and find out. I gently approached her, not wanting to cause any further offense, and posed my question: "Have I done something to you? Why are you sitting in here?"

She said, "I am just resting. I need some time alone."

Her response, though clear, did not register. In a few hours Marlinda emerged from the bedroom bubbly and energetic. I was amazed at the transformation. I've learned that Marlinda's recharging is like Clark Kent going into a telephone booth and emerging as Superman. She's taught me over the years that she recharges by being isolated. Now, after twenty years of marriage, I know what to do when Marlinda is feeling empty and she dashes past me for the nearest telephone booth crying, "I need some Marlinda time." I merely get out of her way, knowing that her time alone will be rewarding and refreshing to her—as well as to me.

When our two children came along, we had to instruct them about our various modes of recharging. Then we taught them how to discover their individual methods of personal renewal. Learning your methods of recharging is important to you and your family. When I tell my children, "Girls, Daddy needs to sit in his study and write," they both quickly exit the room, knowing that my recharging will bring benefits to them and me.

Taking time to recharge your mind, body, and spirit is like putting gasoline into a car's fuel tank. It causes the automobile to run, which enables the driver to get to and from his destination. Your dream can only be realized when your body and mind are energized through restful times.

To discover what brings you rest, think back over the past thirty days as you complete the following exercise.

Discovering What Brings You Rest

What activities within the past 30 days brought you pleasure?	Within 24 hours of the activity, did you say to yourself, "This activity refreshed me"?	Was this a one-time event, or can it be repeated?	How often would you like to repeat this activity?
1.			
2.			
3.			
4.			
5.			

Don't skip over this exercise. If you go through this assignment with honest reflection, you will quickly identify the

secrets of a satisfying life

sources of pleasure in your life. The aim of this exercise is to get you to make a commitment to participating regularly in activities that bring you enjoyment and refreshment. Just as you schedule your business appointments, family functions, and other obligations, you must schedule your reenergizing activities.

At a recent company picnic, I found myself on the softball field playing my old high school position of third base. Although I no longer have the dexterity of a teenager, the old muscles and the old moves came alive. Driving home after the game and picnic had ended, I asked myself, *Why don't I do this more often?* The competitive elements of softball coupled with the jovial interchange with the guys was refreshing. I made a commitment that day to include these kinds of activities in my life. I followed through by joining a gym and committing to participate regularly in competitive activities.

Develop Your Personal Work Style

The key to preserving happiness can be found when you develop a work style that integrates relaxation with busyness. What is your work style? Do you work nonstop and then take a break? Or do you intersperse work with relaxation? This is the place you have to start building a lifestyle of satisfaction because your work style reflects your outlook on life. You must develop this habit today in order to achieve the long-term benefit. Some people wait until retirement before they can start enjoying life, while others believe that every stage in life should have moments of enjoyment. Which category do you fit into?

A college friend once shared with me that while he was growing up, his father would always reprimand him if he wasn't studying or planning for his future. Interestingly, once the father reached retirement age, he apologized to his son, saying, "I'm sorry that I pushed you so hard when you were a child. It's just that I never knew how to relax. And it seemed like having fun was a waste of time." To avoid this trap, you must develop early on the habit of weaving relaxation into your work style.

John Henry Fabre, the great French naturalist, conducted a most unusual experiment with processionary caterpillars. These caterpillars blindly follow the one in front of them—hence their name. Fabre carefully arranged them in a circle around the rim of a flowerpot so that the lead caterpillar actually touched the last one, making a complete circle. In the center of the flowerpot he put pine needles, which is the food of the processionary caterpillar. The caterpillars started around the circular flowerpot.

Around and around they went, hour after hour, day after day, night after night. For seven full days and seven full nights they went around the flowerpot. Finally they dropped dead of starvation and exhaustion. With an abundance of food less than six inches away, they literally starved to death because they confused activity with accomplishment.[3]

Many people make the same mistake and as a result reap only a small fraction of the harvest life has to offer. Despite the fact that untold happiness and satisfaction lies within their reach, they acquire very little of it because they blindly follow the crowd in a lifestyle of excessive busyness. A solid philosophy outlining your work style is needed in order to safeguard your values.

Philosophy seeks to discover the "why" behind one's actions or responses. Why do you have the work style that you do? What is the reason behind your fear of building regular rest periods into your schedule? These questions can guide you through any emotional questions surrounding the adoption of the new habits and will help you live a happier life.

The Ingredient of Flexibility

Two key ingredients that will help you develop a work style that integrates busyness and rest are flexibility and enjoyment. In order for your work to be rejuvenating as well as productive, you have to look at the benefits your work provides. Recognizing your own contributions will spark creativity, which is essential to flexibility and enjoyment. Even when problems arise, creativity emerges from restful periods offering innovative solutions rather than the old methods and styles. Another advantage is that creativity produces new styles, methods, and even flexibility, making your work more enjoyable.

The manager of a large office noticed a new employee and told him to come into the manager's office. "What is your name?" was the first thing the manager asked the new guy.

"Gary," the new guy replied.

The manager scowled, "Look, I don't know what kind of a namby-pamby place you worked at before, but I don't call anyone by their first name. It breeds familiarity, and that leads to a breakdown in authority. I refer to my employees by their last name only: Smith, Jones, Baker. . . . That's all. I am to be referred to only as Mr. Robertson. Now that we've got that straight, what is your last name?"

The new guy sighed, "Darling. My name is Gary Darling."

"Okay, Gary, the next thing I want to tell you is . . ."

Sometimes the old rules don't apply. In such cases, you have to think on your feet, like Mr. Robertson, and become more flexible. Adding this openness to your work style ensures that your goals will not be hampered in any way.

The Ingredient of Enjoyment

You have to enjoy your work style. It's like the story of the man who watched two masons working on a building. He noticed that one worker continually frowned, groaned, and cursed his labors. When asked what he was doing, he replied, "Just piling one stone on top of another all day long until my back is about to break." The other mason whistled as he worked. His movements were swift and sure, and his face was aglow with satisfaction. When asked what he was doing, he replied, "Sir, I'm helping build a cathedral."

A key to enjoying your work, no matter what type of job you're doing, is to appreciate the value it contributes to society. Your contribution to the company for which you work is highly valuable in the grand scheme of things. Just imagine if your company were to eliminate your department or section. What impact would that have on the company's products or effectiveness in serving its clientele? The value you place upon your work must bring you the kind of personal satisfaction the mason who whistled as he worked had. He saw the big picture, and he saw his role as integral to the creation of a fabulous cathedral.

If you are in an unstable job where layoffs are a regular occurrence, worrying or walking around with a depressed look is not going to help any. You must view your role, whether secure or not, as valuable. If you and every other worker on your job strive to improve the organizational culture and increase productivity—regardless of the company's economic stability—it will be an enjoyable place to work. This is precisely the point of developing a work style that includes the element of enjoyment. Work should be enjoyed. People who enjoy what they do for a living and where they work are far happier about their lives.

Enjoy the Process

A man just had his annual physical exam and was waiting for the doctor's initial report. After a few minutes the doctor came in with charts in his hand and said, "There's no reason why you can't live a completely normal life as long as you don't try to enjoy it."[4]

Contrary to the doctor's advice, one of the greatest lessons you can ever learn is to enjoy life through the process of attaining your goals. Granted, attaining your goals brings pleasure. However, connecting rest with busyness gives you a new perspective and enables you to enjoy the ride, not just the final destination.

Have you ever taken a long car ride with small children? They begin asking "Are we there yet?" the moment you pull out of the driveway. Not only is the question annoying, it comes on the heels of your mad dash to pack vacation clothes, toys, gifts, snacks, and so on. Thankfully, some astute engineer has designed modern cars with the ability to play DVD and VHS movies to rear seat passengers. If I had to take a wild guess, I would say that the engineer was a parent of small children. Playing movies in the car allows children *and* their parents to enjoy long rides.

Learn to make the route to your lifelong goals enjoyable. Rest gives you a chance to regroup from the busy pursuit of a dream. Once emotional energy is regained, the destination seems nearer and the view is more picturesque.

Dealing with Other People's Successes

One of the primary enemies of another person's success is envy. Unselfishness says, "I rejoice with those who rejoice and weep with those who weep." This is a great principle to live by because it fosters a spirit of community. The successes of others are to be celebrated, and the failures of others are to be mourned. Beware of envying the successes of others rather than celebrating and being encouraged by their achievements. Coveting someone else's job, house, car, achievements, or spouse is never going to bring you happiness. It will keep you in a constant state of dissatisfaction with your present and prior achievements. Personal joy can be gained and protected when you resist the temptation to compare your level of success to that of others.

If you feel pressured to do a comparison, compare yourself with your destiny. Ask yourself these questions: What is my dream? Can I enjoy what I have today? Am I working for happiness? Am I enjoying the process of achieving my goals? These questions will help you keep a sober perspective on your goals so that you can avoid the lure of comparing.

On his first day of rounds in the psychiatric ward, Dr. Jones was escorted by a seasoned orderly. As Jones walked down the hallway, he heard a man crying at the top of his lungs, "Nancy! Nancy!" As he peered through the glass of the door, he saw that the man within the cell was actually bouncing off the walls while calling out, "Nancy! Nancy!" When he asked the orderly about the man, he replied, "Oh, that's just Fred. He admired this guy's girlfriend, named Nancy. Surprisingly, just two weeks after Nancy broke up with her boyfriend, without hesitation Fred conveyed his feelings toward her. They began dating, and over time their feelings for one another blossomed. However, when Fred asked Nancy to marry him, she said no without offering him a good reason. Fred couldn't handle the rejection, and he just lost it."

They walked on. As they stepped out of the elevator onto the second floor, Dr. Jones heard another man crying out, "Nancy! Nancy!" Through the opening in the door, he saw this man also bouncing off the walls of his room yelling, "Nancy! Nancy!" Dr. Jones asked the orderly, "Why is this man yelling out 'Nancy! Nancy!'?" The orderly replied, "Oh, this is Steve. He's the guy that married Nancy."

The point is well illustrated: the grass actually may *not* be greener on the other side. Comparisons may lead to your demise. Avoid them and enjoy your own successes.

Taking Risks

Another significant deterrent to enjoying the process is an unwillingness to take risks. It is so easy to sit back and sulk about your lack of opportunities, about being in the wrong place at the wrong time, about past mistakes, and about anything else depressing that may come to mind. The bottom line is, you must take risks if you want to enjoy the process of striving for your dream.

One day in July, a farmer sat in front of his shack smoking his corncob pipe. Along came a stranger who asked, "How's your cotton coming?"

"Ain't got none," was the answer. "Didn't plant none. 'Fraid of the boll weevil."

"Well, how's your corn?"

"Didn't plant none. 'Fraid o' drought."

"How about your potatoes?"

"Ain't got none. Scairt o' tater bugs."

The stranger finally asked, "Well, what did you plant?"

"Nothin'," answered the farmer. "I played it safe."[5]

Don't be like this farmer. Without risks you won't have any crops. If you want to harvest your dreams, take risks. You don't have to live on the wild side to take risks. You won't find me bungee jumping or hang gliding, yet I am as big a risk-taker as they come when it has to do with achieving my goals.

When the late Nadine Stair of Louisville, Kentucky, was eighty-five years old, the question was posed to her, "If you had to live your life over, what would you do?" Her response was amazing. She said,

> I'd make more mistakes next time. I'd relax. I would limber up. I would be sillier than I have been this trip. I would take fewer things seriously. I would take more chances. I would climb more mountains and swim more rivers. I would eat more ice cream and less beans. I would perhaps have more actual troubles but I'd have fewer imaginary ones. You see, I'm one of those people who live sensibly and sanely hour after hour, day after day. Oh, I've had my moments, and if I had to do it over again, I'd have more of them. In fact, I'd try to have nothing else. Just moments, one after another, instead of living so many years ahead of each day. I've been one of those persons who never go anywhere without a thermometer, a hot water bottle and a raincoat. If I had to do it over again, I would travel lighter than I have. If I had my life to live over, I would start barefoot earlier in the spring and stay that way later in the fall. I would go to more dances. I would ride more merry-go-rounds. I would pick more daisies.[6]

Like Nadine suggested, why not enjoy the process of living today rather than postponing enjoyment for the winter years of your life? High achievers often overlook rest times as beneficial components for accomplishing their tasks. Their Palm Pilots or personal organizers seldom have a Sabbath day built into the weekly schedule. Yet their calendars have business meetings and teleconferences protected like military outposts. Make the decision right now to integrate rest and busyness so that you can achieve a life of satisfaction.

7

prescription for happy relationships

Most of us rely heavily upon family and friends for moral, emotional, and physical support. How we view these relationships is integral to our state of happiness. A study involving over eight thousand adults concluded that a person's level of happiness is reduced by 26 percent if they regularly compare the quality of their family and social relationships to that of others.[1] Thus we should develop the habit of enjoying and having a realistic view of our family and friends. Creating an artificial standard based on comparisons is counterproductive to achieving satisfaction in life.

The emotional state in our families and critical relationships often establishes our level of satisfaction with our lives. Only the ultra-egotistical person can appear indifferent to unhappiness that stems from relational issues. A master's thesis showed that people have a 30 percent increase in happiness when they have a greater community interaction.[2] In other words, we are social creatures, and when we stay true to our nature of socializing, we become happier. The secret to a satisfying life is not really a secret. The problem is that we Americans are far too busy to recognize that our hectic pace is creating unhappiness. The problem is not the pace but the replacement of meaningful social interaction with a breakneck lifestyle.

This is precisely why sitcoms like *Cheers*, *Seinfeld*, and *Friends* are so popular. The American public is starving for the feelings that friendship communities offer, so we live vicariously by sitting on our couches wishing we had a place, as the theme song for *Cheers* declares, "where everybody knows your name."

In diagnosing the mental health of Americans, psychologists C. Murray and M. J. Peacock concluded that the primary factors in discovering a satisfying life were the number of friends, closeness of friends, closeness of family, and meaningful relationships established with colleagues and neighbors.[3] Since it is impossible to achieve a satisfying life apart from creating happy relationships, we must learn five aspects of relationships, which include: (1) the value of vulnerability; (2) healthy conflict resolution; (3) the power of grace; (4) accepting our differences; and (5) the law of time.

The Value of Vulnerability

A lot of people make the mistake of thinking that vulnerability is a source of weakness. I happen to believe that it is a source of strength. I must admit, this is a paradox. In fact, the greatest demonstration of vulnerability was when God, in Christ, entered into the suffering of humanity through

secrets of a satisfying life

the process of securing our salvation on the cross. As the "Lamb of God," Jesus was on a mission to earth that was all about dying a sacrificial death. As the Lamb, he was destined to be slaughtered, fulfilling the painful words Isaiah used hundreds of years prior to describe the act of atonement: "But he was pierced for our transgressions, he was crushed for our iniquities; the punishment that brought us peace was upon him, and by his wounds we are healed" (Isa. 53:5). Jesus made himself vulnerable to beatings and humiliation in order to secure salvation for the human race.

We devalue vulnerability because we don't understand its importance in establishing meaningful relationships. We too often destroy our own relational base by trampling on the hearts of others who expose their vulnerability during moments designed to enhance the bonds of love.

Lower Your Guard

The word *vulnerability* stems from the Latin *vulner re*, which means "to wound." In a fuller definition, vulnerability means "susceptibility to injury or attack." This means that when people become vulnerable in a relationship, they drop their guard and lower their defenses, leaving themselves susceptible to an attack. The vulnerable person chooses to use inviting words rather than harsh ones. The stern demeanor now is replaced by soft conduct. At this point, since the other person's defenses are down you have a choice of either hurting the person or benefiting from their vulnerability. The wise response is to prize the moment as a meaningful display of sincerity.

Choosing to take the road of insensitivity will automatically cause the vulnerable person's shields to go back up. And when the shields rise, the vulnerable person will likely vow to never expose themselves again, at least not with you. On the other hand, if you choose to embrace the vulnerable person, you gain the rare opportunity to really see their heart and soul. These moments are not predictable. They can occur at any time, whether joyous or sad occasions. There is no set pattern. The one fact is, without moments of vulnerability, you cannot have happy and healthy relationships.

Get a Clear Look

A second definition for the word *vulnerable* is "to be exposed." This meaning gives yet another insight into the value of vulnerability. When people become vulnerable, they offer others a clear look into the reasons behind their behavior, choices, and future desires.

In Paul's letter to the Philippians, he opened his heart with these vulnerable words:

> If anyone else thinks he has reasons to put confidence in the flesh, I have more: circumcised on the eighth day, of the people of Israel, of the tribe of Benjamin, a Hebrew of Hebrews; in regard to the law, a Pharisee; as for zeal, persecuting the church; as for legalistic righteousness, faultless.
>
> But whatever was to my profit I now consider loss for the sake of Christ. What is more, I consider everything a loss compared to the surpassing greatness of knowing Christ Jesus my Lord, for whose sake I have lost all things. I consider them rubbish, that I may gain Christ and be found in him, not having a righteousness of my own that comes from the law, but that which is through faith in Christ—the righteousness that comes from God and is by faith.
>
> Philippians 3:4–9

secrets of a satisfying life

Paul became vulnerable to the Philippians by telling them what he was freely giving up to become a servant of Christ. The apostle was not holding back when he used such graphic language as "I now consider loss" (v. 7) or "I consider them rubbish" (v. 8) in referring to his Hebrew roots and pedigree. The word *rubbish* means dung, waste, or excrement. This man was spelling out his disdain for his natural heritage if it meant choosing that over Christ, his spiritual heritage. If this is not vulnerability, I don't know what is.

When your relationship is moving toward greater levels of vulnerability, get a clear look at your friend's heart. This is where you will find happiness and true intimacy.

Healthy Conflict Resolution

Communication is about understanding someone else's perspective and explaining yourself in such a way that you too will be understood. If the goal is to have happy relationships, resolving conflict is an essential part of the communication process. Attorney Ken Sande provides a four-step process to resolving conflict in his book *The Peacemaker: A Biblical Guide to Resolving Personal Conflict*.[4] The four steps taken directly from the Bible include:

1. Glorify God
2. Take the plank out of your eye
3. Go and show your friend (or spouse) his/her fault
4. Pursue reconciliation and peace

Marlinda and I frequently hold marriage seminars where we teach couples how to resolve conflicts in their marriage. In addition to drawing from our twenty-plus years of marriage and our knowledge of the Bible, we teach these four steps to help people arrive at a harmonious outcome.

1. Glorify God

Glorifying God is an important stance that is not to be compromised by any Bible-believing Christian. Paul writes, "So whether you eat or drink or whatever you do, do it all for the glory of God" (1 Cor. 10:31). Christians are to be unwavering in the goal of living so that God gets glory from everything we do and think. This approach to life helps bring conflict and communication challenges into proper perspective. The focus becomes eternal, which forces us to take on a level of thinking that transcends the earthly and mundane, no matter how painful. The desire to glorify God motivates us to take personal control of our emotions, actions, and decisions.

If you and your friend (or spouse) can't work through your communication challenges, ask yourself the question, "Am I glorifying God in the way I'm dealing with this problem?" I guarantee that the question will not only force you into a period of introspection but also move you to action that ultimately brings glory to God. Even if the action causes you to find a way of compromising with the person who may be at fault, your righteous action shows you are also willing to bring glory to God through humility.

2. Take the Plank Out of Your Eye

The phrase "take the plank out of your eye" originated with Jesus when he taught his disciples by saying, "Why do you look at the speck of sawdust in your brother's eye and pay no attention to the plank in your own eye? How can you say to your brother, 'Let me take the speck out of your eye,' when you yourself fail to see the plank in your own eye? You hypocrite, first take the plank out of your eye, and then you will see clearly to remove the speck from your brother's eye" (Luke 6:41–42). In your quest to resolve a relational conflict, the second step is to look at your own faults and contribution to the conflict before pointing out what your friend has done wrong.

This step forces you to take a cold, hard look at yourself, your own faults, and your shortcomings prior to confronting your friend. Our issues usually look much smaller to us than those of our counterpart. But the words of Jesus are filled with wisdom: first take the plank out of your eye, and then you will see clearly to remove the speck from your brother's eye. The plank in your eye obstructs your view of your relationship and the issues surrounding the conflict. This process helps you along the path of recognizing and admitting your weaknesses and mistakes. As you put this step into practice, your friend (or spouse) will be disarmed and the conflict will be diffused.

3. Go and Show Your Friend His Fault

After the plank is removed from your sight, it's time to move the resolution process along to the third step: go and show your friend his or her fault. This practice originates again from Jesus's words, "If your brother sins against you, go and show him his fault" (Matt. 18:15). What Jesus is asking us to do during times of relational conflict is to lovingly confront the person who hurts us. You confront when the offense is dishonoring of God, damaging to the relationship, destructive to other people, or crippling to the spiritual growth of the parties involved.

Most people have no problem confronting someone who has wronged them. The real problem arises in *how* to confront them. The process is more likely to have a positive outcome if you choose an appropriate time and place for the occasion. Confronting at an inopportune time will be detrimental even if the words are spoken in a respectful and loving manner.

Choose your words beforehand, words that will help you open the heart of your friend because you have anticipated their response. During the conversation, focus on using "I" words rather than "you" words. For example, if Marlinda and I are working through a conflict and I want the outcome to increase the health of our relationship, I will say things like "*I* became angry when you didn't respond to me." This is entirely different than "*You* made me angry when you didn't respond to me." The latter is accusatory, while the former reflects the fact that I am taking complete ownership of my response to her actions. If my response is wrong, it is not her fault; it is my fault. Although this does not excuse her for any wrong action on her part, it does, on the other hand, create a basis for a healthy discussion en route to conflict resolution.

4. Pursue Reconciliation and Peace

The final step in this four-step process of conflict resolution is to pursue reconciliation and peace. Paul's words to the Corinthian Christians pave the way to this approach: "Therefore, if anyone is in Christ, he is a new creation; the old has gone, the new has come! All this is from God, who reconciled us to himself through Christ and gave us the ministry of reconciliation" (2 Cor. 5:17–18). Reconciliation is the relational glue of people in God's kingdom. Pursuing peace is the first and last approach to resolving any and every conflict.

A reconciliatory approach to happy relationships seeks not to dwell on the past. It does not allow incidents to create a wedge in relationships. And certainly reconciliation renounces the idea of punishing or getting even with the offending party. Rather, pursuing reconciliation holds onto unity and love. In a practical way, you may pursue reconciliation by inviting the other person to a social outing. A get-together at the neighborhood diner will go a long way to demonstrating your willingness to bury the past offenses.

Practicing these four steps will assure you a satisfied life because your relationships will be happy. This is God's heart and will concerning you. Pursue it!

The Power of Grace

You are changed forever when you discover a broken aspect of yourself and the grace of God goes to work in your life. One Sunday afternoon I found out from a visiting minister that something was greatly lacking in my life. The discovery occurred when I drove him to his hotel and we sat in the lobby for a few minutes just to recap his weekend of ministry at Christ Church. When I have a guest minister who has a great handle on church structure, order, and corporate vision, I normally ask them, "What can I do to make Christ Church more effective as a local New Testament church?" Alan said, "While I was here this weekend, I felt like the church was a well-oiled machine. All the *t*'s were crossed and the *i*'s dotted. I just have one question: Is there grace here for people to fail?" I thought for a moment, and he and I knew the answer to the question. It was no. I was so passionate about doing a great job as a senior pastor that I did not see this great big area of brokenness in my life and mannerisms. Unconsciously, I was sending signals to everyone around me saying, "I don't tolerate failure. In fact, there is no room for failures around me." My heart was pricked by Alan's question. I saw something about myself that afternoon that sparked an eight-month journey toward understanding God's grace and how it could work in my life. I saw so clearly that when people hung around Jesus—whether they were brilliant or average, rich or getting by, a criminal, prostitute, or a struggling saint—he would make them feel welcomed around him. Somehow I had not allowed God's grace to work in that part of my life that allowed room for people who might not be living up to my expectations or my standards. I had to have an experience of God's grace in the area of my leadership practices.

The word *grace* has several meanings that center around the treatment of others. In fact, some scholars indicate that grace is a two-way word, one which can be used of God and humanity. In regards to God, it implies forgiveness, salvation, regeneration, repentance, and the love of God. In regards to humanity, it implies steadfast love for another human being. This latter meaning is the one I am referring to in discussing our quest to establish happy relationships.

Paul gives us some insight into dealing with relational challenges from a grace perspective. He writes, "Let your conversation be always full of grace, seasoned with salt, so that you may know how to answer everyone" (Col. 4:6). Happy relationships are built on conversation, on the quality of words exchanged from honest hearts. These conversations must be full of grace—full of steadfast love toward another human being. I have seen this grace demonstrated in conversations in two ways. The first is when one person absorbs the other person's shortcomings and imperfections.

The other is when the person dispensing grace looks more closely at the other person's heart and intent, rather than listening to words that may not accurately convey what that person means.

Absorb Your Friend's Shortcomings

At times my attitude is not the best and comes across as caustic—especially toward my wife. One thing that I so appreciate about Marlinda is that she knows when to simply absorb this shortcoming of mine by extending grace. She interprets my actions as stemming from exhaustion, which is almost always true. Similarly, at times I have to absorb my wife's broken areas by the grace of God. We don't keep score, but we are aware that apart from God's grace working in and through our lives, we would never be able to achieve a happy, healthy relationship.

I don't know of any happy, healthy relationships that have achieved that notable status without relying on the grace of God to absorb one another's insufficiencies.

Listen to the Heart, Not the Words

Our conversations can very quickly become emotionally charged. Unless we allow God's grace to aid us in learning how to listen to a person's heart and not necessarily that person's choice of words, our relationships will seldom be healthy or happy. The way people around you can learn to listen to you from this perspective is for you to teach them during times of peace. In other words, when there is no quarrel, have a heart-to-heart time of sharing with your friend. Tell him or her that at times you say things that don't accurately represent what you feel or what you mean and that you're asking them to look at your heart during those times.

In order to have this level of open, honest communication, you must be pretty secure in your person. Part of having a healthy security is the ability to humbly acknowledge your brokenness and need for the grace of another person.

Without grace, you will not move closer relationally to anyone, unless the relationship is one-sided and dysfunctional. We all need the grace of another in order to experience meaningful relationships.

Accepting Our Differences

Extending grace to another acknowledges your mutual differences. God made each of us different from every other. We are not clones. We have unique personalities, cultures, ethnicities, races, and experiences. This is why life and relationships can be exciting and adventuresome. We are on a constant journey toward understanding one another and working through our relational difficulties. That is precisely why God's grace is always necessary.

I recently spent a few days with a precious married couple who was clearly having a tough time in their relationship. The tension between them was quite thick. The husband was spontaneous and happy-go-lucky, a real carefree kind of guy. The wife, on the other hand, was serious, analytical, and formal in her mannerisms. When he wasn't thorough in his instructions or information, she would fill in the blanks. And when she was a bit terse in her dialogue, he would smooth out the conversation with a compassionate remark. To an outsider looking in, this couple appeared to make an excellent team. The only problem was that they did not like each other's imperfections, and they made no bones about it.

The harsh reality was that grace was missing from their relationship. They chose to become annoyed with one another rather than absorb each other's differences, shortcomings, and imperfections. When grace is active in a relationship, mere differences don't divide, they unite. Differences in relationships should not divide or alienate the parties. Differences can be built upon to make the bonds of a relationship stronger.

Marlinda and I have quite a number of differences, yet we have learned to apply grace as a uniting force in our marriage. For example, I like multitasking; she likes doing one thing at a time. When I wake up at 4:00 a.m., I am bright-eyed and want to talk. Marlinda says, "There is absolutely nothing to talk about at 4:00 in the morning." I hate to drive, and I don't like to ask for directions. Marlinda loves to drive and will quickly ask for directions if she needs to. I can fall asleep standing up. Marlinda has trouble falling asleep unless the room is perfectly quiet. I grew up in the hustle and bustle of the Big Apple. Marlinda grew up in a small, quiet town called Pleasantville, New Jersey. When I relax and watch television, I enjoy westerns. Marlinda, on the other hand, rarely watches television, and when she does, it is the Home and Garden channel.

We are different. Yet our differences don't divide us; they unite us. Our differences provide us with a broader approach to the world around us because they offer two different perspectives. A great relationship is not when two perfect people come together. It is when an imperfect pair learns to enjoy and capitalize upon their differences. Let grace work in your relationships, despite your differences.

The Law of Time

How long something takes depends a lot on how much attention we devote to it. Waiting for a bus for twenty minutes can seem like ten years, while cutting a birthday cake can suddenly make us realize that a whole decade has gone by unnoticed. Time, or at least our sense of time, seems like a creative act of human imagination. Saint Augustine seemed to agree. He felt that time had more to do with the soul than with the outside world. "What, then, is time?" asked Augustine. "If no one asks me, I know what it is. [But] if I wish to explain it to him who asks, I do not know."[5]

Time has a way of healing relational mishaps that nothing else could fix. The Bible puts it this way: "He has made everything beautiful in its time" (Eccles. 3:11). The law of time is the acknowledgment that some things will only look different, feel different, and cause a different impact over time. As time lapses, the anger may subside, the pain may decrease, the loss may not hurt as much as it once did. Although time is not the panacea for everything, it certainly heals many maladies that appear irreparable at the outset.

Consider for a moment the painful issues in your life five years ago. How do you see those issues today? Most likely they have paled in comparison to how they first appeared. The law of time was at work over the past five years, bringing perspective to your heart, adjusting the severity of your pain, and applying the required healing salve to your memories. Time is a gift of God. Use it to build happy and healthy relationships. As you do so, this habit will produce satisfaction in your own life.

8

firm thighs
and sharp minds

The book of Ecclesiastes is a great place to start when we think of adopting a new habit to balance our lives. "The Preacher," which is the literal translation of the Greek title of this book, has some priceless teachings for us on the matter of using apparent opposites to begin again in our search for the satisfying life.

Most scholars agree that King Solomon, who was known far and wide as the wisest man of his day, was the author of Ecclesiastes. He likely wrote this book during the "winter" of his life, having gained a valuable perspective on the seasons of life in general. Solomon seems to have discerned that much of life is about seeking a balance between what we often view as opposites.

Of Times and Seasons

Read with me the list of activities the wise man counsels us to balance in Ecclesiastes 3:1–8, which as you can see he set off in poetic style, and then look at his conclusions in verses 9–12:

> There is a time for everything,
>   and a season for every activity under heaven:
> a time to be born and a time to die,
>   a time to plant and a time to uproot,
> a time to kill and a time to heal,
>   a time to tear down and a time to build,
> a time to weep and a time to laugh,
>   a time to mourn and a time to dance,
> a time to scatter stones and a time to gather them,
>   a time to embrace and a time to refrain,
> a time to search and a time to give up,
>   a time to keep and a time to throw away,
> a time to tear and a time to mend,
>   a time to be silent and a time to speak,
> a time to love and a time to hate,
>   a time for war and a time for peace.

What does the worker gain from his toil? I have seen the burden God has laid on men. He has made everything beautiful in its time. He has also set eternity in the hearts of men; yet they cannot fathom what God has done from beginning to end. I know that there is nothing better for men than to be happy and do good while they live.

As you can see, the wise man was a student of life—a philosopher, if you will. Don't let the word philosophy frighten you, for the Bible is not only a book of "good news" about how to come to God through Jesus Christ and a book of doctrine, moral truth, and powerful narratives. Scripture is also a book of religious philosophy—teaching that informs our "worldview" by *God's* view, giving us a divine way of looking at life. This passage invites us to get inside the mind of God and learn, among other things, the essential elements or seasons of life and how to balance them even when they seem at odds with each other. That's what Solomon is dealing with here.

When we stop to count them, we find fourteen different couplets, or dual expressions, describing various seasons or activities of life in Ecclesiastes 3:1–8. The fact that many of these couplets seem to be opposites, requiring us to balance them, shows us both the harmony and the ambiguity of life. Solomon does not shy away from presenting the tension between life's dualities.

Tension isn't necessarily negative; it can be good for us. For example, I can experience a certain tension between my roles as a husband and a father. I have to balance the tension of spending quality time both with my wife and with my children. But that's not a negative thing. When I hold these roles in tension with each other, I do a better job as both a husband and a father than I would do if I simply abandoned one role while tending to the other. This kind of healthy tension can lead to stronger families and a more satisfying life.

So when Solomon outlines these fourteen dual facts of life, he invites us to benefit from his experience and wisdom in living with a healthy tension between what could pull us apart and what holds our lives together. The apostle Paul depicts the role of Christ as the "glue" that holds such opposite but essential things together in this way, a role he held even before he came to earth as Jesus of Nazareth. Paul says that Christ "is before all things, and in him all things hold together" (Col. 1:17).

Many people get themselves in jams that show how desperately they need this spiritual "glue." As Shakespeare said, their times "are out of joint." For example, the "generation gap" we hear so much about often results when people in their sixties or seventies are living in the same household as teenagers. The outlooks of each group can be harmonized only when everyone in the home respects each other and refrains from deciding that one season of life is just "wrong." Actually, what is wrong is the way we sometimes fail to harmonize the natural traits of each season of life, becoming loving and accepting of each.

Often we don't like the season of life we're in at the moment. Young people often want to be older, and older people wish they were younger; a bachelor wishes he were married, and a married man wishes he were single. Again, while there are no easy answers here, we can go a long way toward enjoying life when we accept our season as a part of the world that God created and called "good" (as he did several times in Genesis 1).

We often see people who don't particularly like their personality type. If you've ever taken one of the popular personality profiles, you may have come out feeling "labeled" because the test proved that you are, in fact, an "extrovert" or an "introvert," or that you have this tendency or that. I think it's important to remember that when God called his creation "very good," he included personality types as well as "seasons of life." Of course we can make small changes within the boundaries of our personalities and become happier people and perhaps easier to live with. But if we set out to completely change from the kind of person God made us, we can find ourselves in big trouble. When we wrench a basic personality type into something other than what it was designed to be, we can literally get bent out of shape.

Personalities, like seasons of life, are a part of the world as God created it. Let's enjoy who we are, just as we enjoy the seasons of life, instead of wishing we were this or that other kind of person.

I see in Solomon's teaching at least three important secrets that can go a long way in enabling us to begin living a more satisfying life. As we discuss them, I invite you to embrace both ends of the spectrum these dualities cover, because as the wise man said, God "has made everything beautiful in its time" (Eccles. 3:11). Both ends of each couplet have a place in our lives.

The Natural and the Spiritual

In verses 9–11 of Ecclesiastes 3, Solomon hints at the tension between the natural and the spiritual. Although the writer is dealing with the issue of work instead of with the emotional quality of life, he raises the same issue, the same need for balance. For he asks, "What does the worker gain from his toil? I have seen the burden God has laid on men" (vv. 9–10).

In other words, the wise man admits that work, viewed from only a natural standpoint, can be a burden. This fact shouldn't come as a surprise to anyone who has had to toil and labor at work they don't particularly like. Labor can be a burden. Yet the potential for balancing this hard fact of life is in the very next verse, where the writer introduces the possibility of a "spiritual" aspect of work by saying that God "has made everything beautiful in its time" (v. 11).

So often a person's career can infect all of life with tension. A salesman struggles to meet his quota, only to have the quota raised for the next year. On the other hand, some people have jobs which seem so boring and repetitive and to offer so little opportunity for creativity that they too have difficulty seeing how God can make anything "beautiful" out of their work. No wonder we ask with the wise man, "What does the worker gain from his toil?" (v. 9).

Let me give you just one small example of someone who has learned to answer that question positively. The son of a friend of mine took a job at a tool and die firm to earn money for college. The boy was of a decidedly "spiritual" disposition and at first found his job of sorting and storing tools to be so "non-spiritual." Soon, though, this same boy felt that the job was so monotonous that he could have gone crazy with boredom.

Then an older man on the job told him a secret. "Just think how working with your hands at a repetitive job frees your mind to do its own work," the man said. And sure enough, the boy was able to take that small bit of advice to heart. He began to memorize Scripture passages that he typed on note cards and carried in his shirt pocket. He would allow his mind to tussle with moral and spiritual questions while handing out tools to the workmen. Don't misunderstand—he wasn't in a dream world or "so spiritually minded that he was of no earthly good." He was able to do all this mental work without detracting from what was otherwise a mechanical and boring job. And sure enough, he earned enough money for his schooling. He learned to make that job "beautiful in its time."

To illustrate this principle in another way, I often see people, especially young people, who come to Christ with the fervor of spiritual commitment burning so brightly that they are blinded to "natural" realities and, sadly, to their own detriment. The Bible refers to this stage as being a "babe" in Christ (1 Cor. 3:1). This stage is characterized by a sudden burst of excitement and euphoria for the things of God. But I've seen this commendable spiritual emphasis quickly eclipse such natural matters as completing one's education. I've seen babes in Christ suddenly quit pursuing their "secular" studies and devote themselves wholly to studying the Bible. Although they had been "A" students at school, they dropped to "C" students after dedicating their lives to Christ. Their excuse is that they are spending much of their time in spiritual pursuits, such as prayer, fasting, Bible studies, and evangelism.

Similarly, I've seen adult businessmen and businesswomen come to faith in Christ and suddenly give up the drive, courage, and tenacity that had made them excel in business. They lose their aggressiveness in seeking new clients. They let their competitors walk all over them. Does becoming a babe in Christ require that a person become less than professional in his or her job? Not at all! Becoming a Christian, adopting a spiritual worldview, should bring *balance* to one's natural aptitude in business.

I don't want to sound as if I am putting down the joy and even euphoria of being a babe in Christ. However, what I want to point out is that by applying the wisdom of Solomon, we can balance both "secular" and "spiritual" matters. Becoming a Christian should deepen and mature our life skills rather than render them shallow or "beneath us" and unworthy of our time. The spiritual and the natural can cohabit within us *because God is the author of both.* And keeping them in tension with each other can enhance both aspects instead of causing us to neglect one or the other.

The Body and the Spirit

A second principle imbedded in Solomon's fourteen couplets is that truly happy people live in two realms at the same time. They have a spirit which is housed in a body. The truly happy person is writing a poem, pedaling a bicycle, engaged in worship and Bible reading, chasing pests out of the garden, fishing in the neighborhood pond, wrestling in the backyard with the kids, singing in the choir, or taking a daughter to lunch. In other words, the happy person has formed a habit of integrating activities that use the mind and body. We are physical beings that have creative minds. Both of these need exercise in order to stay alert and in good shape. When our bodies are given regular exercise, we feel good about our shape and appearance. Similarly, when our minds and souls receive repeated stimulation, we enjoy our inner lives and others value our company. My point is, God made us to fit into two worlds simultaneously—the natural and spiritual worlds. We must give ourselves equally to activities in both these realms if we are to live satisfying lives.

As a Christian, I find that my faith provides me with answers to address the innumerable dichotomies in this world. I find peace in reading the Bible and turning to God in prayer when pondering heart-wrenching tragedies, wicked actions by malicious people, and even my own shortcomings. In a 1998 study, clinical psychologists J. Gerwood, M. LeBlanc, and N. Piazza observed that people who held strongly to a religious orientation, regardless of the particular religion, lived a more satisfying life.[1] Equally true are the social data pointing to the life satisfaction attributed to exercise. In the book *Fit to Lead*, the authors document that "individuals who are fit are also less likely to become obese and more likely to possess higher levels of energy and enjoy enhanced feelings of well being."[2] They also note that fit individuals tend to enjoy psychological benefits including levels of anxiety, depression, tension, and stress lower than others within society.

It's Not Either-Or

Life will be unfulfilling if we simply give ourselves entirely to activities lying either in the spiritual realm *or* to those in the natural realm. Don't get me wrong; both realms are important. They have both been created by God. God created our bodies. In fact, concerning the body God says, "Do you not know that your body is a temple of the Holy Spirit, who is in you, whom you have received from God? You are not your own; you were bought at a price. Therefore honor God with your body" (1 Cor. 6:19–20). When we ignore the value and importance of our bodies, we suffer great loss that leads to great dissatisfaction in life. Ignoring the body will cause sickness, bodily malfunctions, and a deterioration of our ability to function in the physical realm. Ignoring the body also shows dishonor to God, since giving it the proper attention reflects honor. In short, dishonoring our bodies negatively impacts the way we demonstrate our love and devotion to our Creator. Dishonoring our bodies will not only create physical limitations but also impact our spiritual activities and desires. Although we are singular beings, we exist in both realms, and our existence connects the realms.

As a pastor, I have to maintain a strong anointing on my life in order to impact people through my preaching gift. Strong anointing is brought about through my regular times of prayer and fasting and through living a consistent Christian life. But there is more to it than that. Many years ago, I discovered that some of my best sermons were preached after a full night's rest. Having my body well rested and given the proper physical care affected the way I delivered the eternal Word of God. My experience gave me another reason to value the reality of Paul's words: "honor God with your body" (1 Cor. 6:20).

Six-Pack Abs Underneath Spiritual Armor

The Scriptures call for every Bible-believing Christian to put on the whole armor of God (see Eph. 6:10–18). These are spiritual armaments that protect us against the wiles of our archenemy, Satan. Imagine taking off your spiritual armor to show off your six-pack abs. What a sight! The term "spiritual armor" alongside the descriptive term "six-pack abs" almost seems like an oxymoron. How many Christians engaged in the age-old spiritual battle can boast the fact that they have six-pack abs or enjoy overall health? I know some believers who have impressive abs but are powerless against the devices of the devil. I also know some other saints who can scare the devil because they are so powerful in God but look like the poster child for the overeaters' club. I won't tell you where I fall in this range, but suffice it to say, I am not where I used to be. I'm making impressive strides toward the middle ground—physically fit *and* spiritually battle ready.

We are not just physical beings. We are spirit beings housed in physical bodies. When God breathed the breath (spirit) of life into Adam, Adam became a living being (see Gen. 2:7). Consequently, true life comes from our indwelling spirit. To live the God-kind of life—a satisfied life—ongoing spiritual communion with God and a physically active life are needed. Some people live totally for physical pleasures and physical rewards, while others live totally for spiritual pleasures and spiritual rewards. The physical rewards deal with the here and now, while the spiritual rewards deal mainly with the hereafter. If I had to choose between the two, I would choose the eternal rewards—heaven, God, salvation, and so on. But we are not called to make a choice. We are called to keep *both* activities as a high priority in *this* life.

Natural and Spiritual Living

Sometimes we Christians look down our noses in a self-righteous way at those who run marathons, exercise regularly, rock climb, and go skiing because we think they seem so carnal and self-absorbed. And sometimes they are. But the flip side—the overemphasis of spiritual and religious activity to the neglect of physical needs—is equally dangerous if you're seeking to attain a satisfying life.

I have never done a technical study on this, but from my observation, church people appear to be very physically unhealthy. Many of our social and fellowship-oriented activities center around food—the wrong kinds of food. In my congregation I had to strongly insist that my staff and hospitality department serve healthy cuisine during conferences or other events which involve food. While the health buffs among them were excited about my request, others took months to work out what "healthy" meant. It took so long because many staff members had to *unlearn* years of bad church eating habits. I insisted on fresh fruits rather than the traditional cookies and pastries for dessert. For a particular breakfast meeting, I requested hard-boiled eggs and vegetables rather than the all-time favorite of bagels, muffins, and coffee.

I must admit, when I turned into a health-conscious pastor, my staff quickly realized that my newfound zeal for proper food choices spilled over onto them. It was like going to the mall with a budget-conscious person when all you like to do is spend, spend, spend. Conviction was in the air whenever food was mentioned. Fortunately, two things occurred which lightened the atmosphere. First, I let my actions and choices, not my words, be the sermon. Second, when the benefits of my change became obvious (I lost some fifty pounds over a year and was physically transformed), I made sure to let staff members invite a dialogue about my health choices and new lifestyle decisions.

We all know how America is digging its grave with a knife and fork, but we need to see that from a spiritual and physical perspective, healthy living is a form of godliness. Now, we still have a greater need to spiritually live for God. Both truths need to be preached and heard by each of us if we want to achieve satisfying lives personally and for our family and friends. The balance between the spiritual and natural world must be worked out so that the tension is a positive rather than a negative.

A woman once came to me seeking help for an awkward time of her life. Like many parents these days, she was experiencing some difficulty in her relationship with her children. "Pastor," she said, "my children dislike me. They despise me. I'm doing all I know to do. I fast and I pray all the time, and. . . ." I interrupted her to say, "There's your problem right there."

She was shocked, to say the least. Here I was, her pastor, telling her that the problem was that she was spending too much time in fasting and prayer. Since I'm entirely in favor of fasting and praying, I hastened to explain. "What I'm suggesting," I said, "is that you may be spending so much time in spiritual disciplines that you're neglecting some very down-to-earth things that would help you relate to your children. The best advice I can offer you is that you go home and bake some chocolate chip cookies or that you take time to play some board games with your children."

I will be the first to affirm that a mother's relationship with members of her family can be enhanced by fasting and prayer. But this woman was engaging in explicitly "spiritual" matters to the neglect of "natural" ways of relating to her children. The spiritual and the natural are not mutually

secrets of a satisfying life

exclusive. They each have their own contribution to make in the balanced Christian life.

The Earthly and the Eternal

Solomon's profound list of the various seasons of life contains a third principle that we need to keep in balance: the tension between the earthly, or temporal, and the eternal. In Ecclesiastes 3:11 he says that God "has also set eternity in the hearts of men; yet they cannot fathom what God has done from beginning to end."

Here's another duality that many people give up on because it can be difficult: we are to keep a strong grip on earthly things while also maintaining our grasp on things eternal. Let me illustrate from a time in my own life when I had trouble maintaining this balance. I became a Christian while I was studying engineering. I was caught up in books about thermodynamics and circuit systems and calculus and differential equations—all of it pretty heady stuff. Then along came my conversion experience, and I began my theological studies with equal seriousness. I read books on the doctrine of God, the doctrine of man, hermeneutics, homiletics—all the usual seminary stuff.

After I began to pastor a church, a friend asked me one day, "Pastor, do you ever read fun books?"

"What do you mean, 'fun books'?" I responded. You see, I had become so caught up in all this "eternally heavy" reading, first in engineering and then in theology, I had forgotten that it was okay to just read stuff for fun! I'd forgotten that such things existed. And when I finally allowed myself to get into some of the lighter books my friend gave me, I actually felt guilty. I wasn't reading for the purpose of solving eternal matters. I was having fun!

You see this same syndrome sometimes when people who have led the life of a "party animal" become Christians. Suddenly they're plunged into confronting the eternal—really serious stuff about right and wrong, heaven and hell. They become so doggedly serious that they don't have time to celebrate the joy of being in Christ! They think, *I don't have time for that joy business. I have to grow in the Lord. I have to study and learn.*

If this kind of person isn't careful, he can simply trade one dysfunctional behavior for another. A person who is merely a party animal is dysfunctional in the realm of the eternal. But a person who totally gives up the spirit of celebration is dysfunctional in the realm of the temporal or the earthly.

One of the amazing things about the early Christians is that they were characterized by joy in the midst of persecutions, while surrounded on every side by the very serious possibility of losing their lives. From a prison cell, staring eternity in the face, the apostle Paul wrote, "Rejoice in the Lord always. I will say it again: Rejoice!" (Phil. 4:4). Here Paul was reflecting a firm grip on both eternity and the earthly matters at hand.

The fact is, as Solomon understood so well, believers must keep one foot firmly planted in eternity and the other on earth. This healthy personality makes them not schizophrenic but balanced. The most effective Christians are those who keep a strong grip on this world and a strong hope in the next. This kind of balance is absolutely essential if we are to navigate the seasons of life successfully. Ironically, only those with a firm sense of eternity can make their way through the confusion and perplexity of this life.

As I talk with people, I often see signs that they are neglecting one of these poles or the other. Some people can't tell me enough about their success in the business world.

They've just been promoted, they've been named top sales-man, they've expanded their business—in short, they are a resounding success by every measuring stick the world has to offer. Then I move the conversation to issues such as their prayer life, their spiritual growth, their devotion to the work of the church, and they are strangely quiet. They have apparently gained a strong grip on the temporal at the expense of the eternal.

But equally disturbing to me are Christians who can speak of nothing other than their involvement in the things of the Spirit. "I'm growing in the Spirit as never before," they'll say. "I pray and I read my Bible regularly, my daily devotions are so rich, and I never miss a church service." And then they'll let it slip that their marriage is breaking up, or that things at work are lousy, or that they actually hate their boss.

Or I'll ask, "Did you vote yesterday in the race for mayor?" and they'll say, "Oh, I don't bother with voting. I leave those things of the world to someone else."

Do you see what's going on here? A false attachment to what we've learned to categorize as "eternal" has blinded us to the importance of what we've learned to dismiss as "earthly." We must learn from Solomon that both of these entities are essential aspects of life, both are poles of the same reality: life under the rule of God.

Sometimes our dysfunction in these areas shows up in the way we try to avoid "earthly" issues by getting caught up in unanswerable or abstract questions. For example, I frequently talk to people who just can't let go of the old question of whether animals have souls. "Sure they do," they'll argue. "Doesn't the Bible say that the lamb and the lion will lie down together?" Or they'll argue without end about what kind of body we'll have in heaven or about the nature of hell ("How can it be a place of total darkness if the fire never burns out or is quenched?"). Another favorite question is where Cain and Abel got their wives . . . and on and on we can go, asking questions that keep us distracted with the "eternal"—by which here I mean unanswerable! Then our spouse will ask, "Honey, will you take out the garbage?" or, "Honey, I need you to go the store for me, okay?" And suddenly we're rudely brought down to earth—where we need to be, since we happen to live here! And we realize that we've tried to hide from such "small" and earthly realities behind "huge" and eternal questions. We need to realize that we can be enormously successful at fixing our minds on abstractions and yet fail in the natural areas of being a husband, father, wife, or mother.

Yes, God *has* "set eternity in the hearts of men." But he hasn't condescended to answer all our questions about it! Then what can we do about all those unanswered and unanswerable questions? We can take out that insurance policy he has provided—we can place our trust in Jesus Christ, who is eternal and who lived for a time on the earth. Then, to take care of earthly reality, we can be sure to get a life insurance policy on ourselves so that our family will be taken care of if God decides to rush eternity upon us while they're still dealing with earthly realities. That's the kind of balance the wise man is urging us to keep. Both earth and eternity are "seasons" that are essential to tend to. We dare not neglect either dimension.

9

the habit of forgiveness

Achieving a satisfying life goes beyond the external creature comforts to include having a satisfying inner life. A satisfied life is a life filled with the practice of forgiveness. Living with unforgiveness is like walking around with a ton of bricks on your back. While many have developed strong backs by hanging onto their bitterness and resentment, happy people enjoy the benefits that forgiveness brings.

Although academic interest in person-to-person forgiveness is relatively new, former President Jimmy Carter, Archbishop Desmond Tutu, and former missionary Elisabeth Elliot are leading a $10 million "Campaign for Forgiveness Research." In May 1998 the John Templeton Foundation awarded research grants to twenty-nine scholars for the study of forgiveness. The research findings include the observation that giving and receiving forgiveness is necessary to having and maintaining healthy relationships.

The apostle Peter took note of Jesus as a gentle and forgiving person. And in an effort to endear himself to the Master, he asked, "Lord, how many times shall I forgive my brother when he sins against me? Up to seven times?" (Matt. 18:21).

In response, Jesus told the story of a debtor who was brought before the king, to whom he owed the huge debt of 10,000 talents (Matt. 18:23–34). Since he couldn't pay up, the king ordered that he be put in the debtor's prison and that his wife and children and all that he owned be sold and the proceeds applied to the debt. But the debtor made a moving plea to be forgiven of his debt, and the king took pity on him, canceled his debt, and let him go free.

What happened next? The forgiven servant went out and found a fellow servant who owed him a measly debt of 100 denarii. When this man couldn't pay either, the first servant had the second thrown into the very prison from which he had been spared. And when the king found out that the one to whom forgiveness had been shown had in turn proven himself to be unforgiving, the king consigned the first debtor to prison after all. Jesus concludes the story with an application to our relationship with God and those who wrong us: "This is how my heavenly Father will treat each of you unless you forgive your brother from your heart" (Matt. 18:35). This famous parable shows the tremendous power of the past—both over those who suffer at the hands of the unmerciful and over unmerciful people themselves.

Perspectives on Breaking Chains

Jesus's parable shows that the way we unlock the chains of our past is to seek God's forgiveness *and* the forgiveness of those we have hurt. It also shows how those who have been hurt can loose the chains that have bound them in anger, blame, and grudge-bearing.

But it's easier said than done, isn't it?

We need to realize that no matter how much we have hurt others in our past, we have hurt God more. Sometimes circumstances make it impossible to gain forgiveness from others, but God is always available to forgive us of the greater debt we owe to him. This is why your goal of achieving a satisfying life must incorporate the habit of practicing forgiveness.

Incorporating this habit into your lifestyle requires that you gain the proper perspective on those who may have hurt you and those whom you may have hurt. The wicked servant in Jesus's parable owed the king, who represents God, 10,000 talents. That would be somewhere around *$1 billion* in our present currency. (And my kids sometimes get upset when I owe them a quarter!) This servant owed so much that selling his wife and children wouldn't even settle the debt. In those days you might get anywhere from 500 to 2,000 denarii for a slave, which wouldn't even amount to 1 percent of what the wicked servant owed his master. On the other hand, his fellow servant owed him only 100 denarii, which would be about $1,000 in our money. There's no comparison! And the great irony in the parable is that the wicked servant was willing to have *his* debtor thrown into prison for $1,000 when he himself had just been forgiven a $1 billion debt.

The point here is that you can allow an unforgiving spirit to keep you in a spiritual debtor's prison over an incredibly minor infraction that someone has committed against you in the past—a debt that shrinks to nothing when compared to the huge debt of rebellion and disobedience for which God is willing to forgive you.

The question you must ask yourself is this: *Is it worth it to hold onto my grudge and allow it to bind me to the past when I've been forgiven of so much more?*

The family is one of the most urgent arenas in which we need to apply this parable. I cannot tell you how many people I talk to who have allowed little hurts and slights by family members to give their homes the oppressive atmosphere of a "debtor's prison." They are chained to past hurts and past infractions.

A story is told of a father in Spain who disciplined his teenage son, Paco, for being incredibly rude and disrespectful. In response the boy stormed out of the house, vowing never to return. He didn't show up that night, so his father called the boy's friends and spent the next few days searching for him, putting the word out that he wanted to be reconciled with his son. But his efforts were fruitless.

Finally, the father put an advertisement in the newspaper in Madrid. In it he made an impassioned plea to Paco, begging him to return. "Dear Paco," the ad said, "All is forgiven. Come back home, son. Let's put this behind us. Let's forgive each other and work through this. Meet me at the newspaper stand tomorrow at noon. I'll see you there, Paco. Love, Dad."

At noon on the day the ad appeared, eight hundred boys named Paco showed up at the newspaper stand!

I wonder what family member in your life needs your forgiveness. I wonder what they may have done to you, how they wounded or battered you, what they may have said to you that so cut you in your spirit that you have felt alienated and bound by the chains of the past, perhaps for years. The message of Jesus is that *they* are bound too and need your forgiveness. Can you allow the power of Jesus to enable you to extend forgiveness to them, thus releasing both your family member and yourself from those chains?

Can't you see that the thousand-dollar debt they may owe you is nothing when compared with the billion-dollar debt Christ has canceled for you?

We really don't need to allow the debt among family members to build up to this enormous size. Living together in a family by nature involves some bumping into each other. Living in a family requires an *attitude* of forgiveness that is ongoing, that keeps the little slights and offenses that commonly occur from building up. Living in a family requires forgiveness on a regular basis, lest the family degenerate or atrophy.

Our families will fall apart unless we recognize the wisdom of God and access the courage of God in order to say, "I forgive you." How many times? Well, Peter thought he was being very gracious in suggesting that he might conceivably be able to forgive a brother seven times. Jesus bursts his bubble by saying, "How about seventy-seven times?" (or, as the older versions have it from some manuscripts, "seventy times seven"; see Matt. 18:22). Picture Peter crunching the numbers on his calculator (or maybe an abacus?) and coming up with not seven incidents of forgiveness but 490 incidents!

Obviously Jesus is not talking about a specific figure but about the posture we ought to have when it comes to the topic of forgiveness. He's speaking of an attitude, not the ability to keep score. He's talking about the way we shape our lives. You don't live in obedience to this teaching by keeping a record and thinking, "Well, I've forgiven my brother 482 times. Just eight more wrongs and then I can stop forgiving him!"

God's Forgiving Nature

Jesus's parable, which shows the way we should forgive, is based on the nature of a forgiving God. Think about all the sins you've committed and all the times he has forgiven you. Of course, you *can't* really do this because you aren't even aware of all the times you've committed an affront against God. You've been sinning since you were a baby, since before you saw that your infant sister had a bottle in her mouth and you knocked it out because you wanted it! In a few years you were stealing your brother's chewing gum . . . and then when he complained to your parents, you lied and said you didn't steal it! But God was there all the time, just waiting to forgive you like the great king in the parable.

I am reminded of the story of the little boy whose parents had just given their lives to Christ. When they sent their little Johnny to the Christian day care center the next day, the children were learning the Bible story of Joshua. The teacher asked the group, "Who broke down the walls of Jericho?" Little Johnny answered, "Not me! I didn't do it! I'm new to this school. Don't blame me for it!" At the end of the day, when little Johnny's father came to pick him up, the teacher reported the incident to him. The father said, "Look, if my son said he didn't do it, he didn't do it! But we're new to this neighborhood and I want to get off to a good start, so if it turns out that he did, I'll pay for the damages!"

Our God stands that ready to forgive us, to pay the debts we owe—although he's much better informed than little Johnny's dad. This readiness to forgive extends both to our deliberate sins and to the sins of which we are not aware. The New Testament word for sin simply means "missing the mark," as when an archer makes a poor shot. All of us fail at some time or another to hit the bull's-eye of God's standards in how we live our lives. But we trust the living God, who allows continuous contact with the forgiving blood of Christ to enable us not only to *ask* for forgiveness but to *live* in forgiveness (see 1 John 1:7). We see again that forgiveness depends more on the nature of God than it does on our ability to recall and seek forgiveness for every "arrow" we've misdirected. But, of course, not everyone understands the forgiving nature of God. We don't always understand the power of our acting, as believers, on the basis of God's nature and thus releasing the incredible power of forgiveness.

Those things in life others have done that have hurt you and those derogatory comments that were unfairly said about you or to you naturally create sore spots. Unfortunately, when we fail to allow the nature of a forgiving God to enable us to forgive, we can be among the walking wounded, carrying those sores around with us and allowing them to cripple us for years. Yet we have counted on God to forgive us. This parable essentially asks, "*In light of how God has forgiven you, isn't it time to forgive those who hurt you?*" If you choose not to forgive, you're going to walk around crippled, even though you believe in a God of healing. You're going to interact with others out of resentment and hatred, even though you worship a God whose nature is love. And unforgiveness will keep you in a constant state of dissatisfaction. You'll be dissatisfied with people, with yourself, and perhaps even with God. Forgiveness is one of the secret doorways that leads to a satisfying life.

Have you ever experienced the freedom either of forgiving another person or of *being* forgiven yourself? It's a "high" that's available to those who are willing to reflect the nature of God in the way they deal with others.

A few years ago our church owed a radio station a considerable debt. We had been broadcasting in a prime-time slot but had discontinued our program when we decided to give greater emphasis to the refurbishing of our facilities. We left the air owing the station approximately $10,000. We were determined to be responsible with the repayment, but we were paying off the debt a little at a time. One day one of the vice presidents of the radio station came to church for a service at which we dedicated our refurbished facilities. I noticed him in the audience, and he seemed to be enjoying the service. But I wasn't prepared for what he said to me after the service.

"Pastor Ireland," he said, "I want you to know that we're writing off that $10,000 debt that you've been working at paying off. Just forget about it. It's over."

Now, I want to tell you that in that moment I experienced the presence of God! We may think that our hearts aren't linked to money, and as a pastor I like to think that I don't worry that much about finances. But all you have to do to correct this misconception is to think about not having to pay $10,000 and about someone else putting aside a claim on $10,000! I'm telling you, this man's word of forgiveness for a $10,000 debt made an impression on me.

Who is the person in your life that is waiting for a similar experience? Perhaps it has nothing to do with money, but they're waiting for you to indicate such a forgiving attitude toward them.

What Forgiveness Is Not

Forgiveness can be tricky. Because it's a part of the character of God, believers want to be known as forgiving persons. But sometimes we go about it in ways that belie what forgiveness really is.

Ignoring the Problem

Forgiveness isn't ignoring the wrongs we have experienced. The Christian must not be like Linus in the *Peanuts* comic strip. He and Charlie Brown are walking along one day, and Linus turns to Charlie Brown and says, "I just hate problems, and one of the ways I deal with them is I just ignore them."

secrets of a satisfying life

Then a little later he expands on the idea and adds, "There's no problem so hard or so complicated that it can't be ignored."

Well, that sometimes seems to be the route we take—the easy way out. The problem is that it doesn't work. You wonder why you're at odds with your wife and you snap at her for no apparent reason? Look into the past for some of those chains. You may be responding in the present to a wound out of the past—one that you've been failing to deal with, trying to ignore it, like Linus.

Can you imagine how deeply Christ was hurt by knowing in advance that Peter would deny him? Jesus could have much more easily ignored Peter's approaching faithlessness. But instead of taking Linus's approach, Jesus both dealt with the problem ("Before the rooster crows today, you will deny three times that you know me"; Luke 22:34) and extended his compassion and forgiveness ("When you have turned back, strengthen your brothers"; Luke 22:32).

"Feeling" like Forgiving

Forgiveness at its fullest involves an act of the heart. But sometimes we must forgive even when we don't feel like it. Holding a grudge is too costly. If you don't face the issue of forgiveness directly, it will work on the inside and wound you. On the other hand, an abundance of evidence shows the positive results of *not* ignoring the issue.

Some time ago I was speaking to a gentleman who was in his late fifties but looked as though he was in his early seventies. I asked him, "What's gone on in your life? You seem somehow to have been held captive emotionally. Do you want to talk about it?"

He looked at me, then dropped his head for a moment and said, "You know, fifteen years ago I was so bitter. I was

---

the habit of forgiveness

angry at my wife. I was angry at my children. I was angry at my co-workers. I was angry at the world. I had so much bitterness in my heart, I had so much resentment, and as a result I had a lot of different sicknesses. I had leukemia. I had blood problems. I had sugar diabetes. I contracted so many different illnesses that I had all these knots in my stomach."

He continued, "One day I was so sick that I had to be taken to the hospital in an ambulance. And there, on my hospital bed, I was sure I was about to die. I was still angry. As I lay there, all I could think about was the way people had hurt me. But it was there on my deathbed that I heard the voice of the Holy Spirit speak to me. He said to me, 'Can you forgive them? *Will* you forgive them?'"

The man told me that at that moment of despair, when he thought he was going to slip into eternity, he simply said to God, "Lord, I ask you to help me forgive them." He couldn't do it on his own. But he said that by faith he forgave his wife, his children, his co-workers, and all those who had hurt him throughout the years.

"The moment I said that I forgave them by faith," he said, "it was like a ton of bricks had fallen right off of me. In a couple of days I was released from the hospital."

This happened all because he forgave! You see, the word *forgive* means to set free, to release. It's a judicial act. To forgive means that somehow you have released from the prison of your heart those whom you've held captive for their misdeeds toward you. To keep them prisoners for very long is too costly. They become a drain on you, the jailor. So even if you don't have a completely forgiving spirit, you have to set them free, both for their sake and for yours. Even if the only forgiveness you can offer is an act of faith, you must set them, and yourself, free.

Think about it: this ability to set someone free, even when we don't feel like forgiving, is one of the greatest gifts God has given us. An act of faith is something no one can take from you. No one can say to you that you *can't* forgive someone. You can be in a prison but set someone else free in your heart. You can be poor but forgive someone lavishly.

And forgive we must. For when we don't, we ourselves are the real prisoners. The probability of living a satisfied life is drastically less for a prisoner than for those who have full freedom. When you consider the costs, practicing forgiveness is the surefire route to take if achieving a satisfying life is your goal.

How to Let Go of the Past

We must not be naïve in our insistence on forgiving. Some wounds go so deep that letting go of the hurt and resentment is difficult. We can be amazingly quick to harbor a hurt. We cling to the smallest slight, partly out of pride. We want the other person to have the forgiving spirit while we insist on remembering that we were in the right and they were in the wrong.

Value Reconciliation over Being Right

Sometimes we punish ourselves by reminding ourselves that *we* are the offended party and that the other person was wrong. But think about it: sometimes it's better to be reconciled than it is to be right.

Imagine a man and his wife having an argument. She says something harsh that enrages her husband. At bedtime, instead of sleeping in bed with her, he snatches up a blanket and storms out of the bedroom. He resolves to sleep on the couch. She asks him to forgive her and to come to bed, but nothing she says convinces him to forgive her for what she carelessly said. He'd rather keep his pride than be reconciled with his wife. "Sir," I want to say to him, "wouldn't it be better to be reconciled with your wife than to be right and have to sleep on that lumpy old couch?"

Or imagine a child who commits a small act of disrespect toward her mother. The mom storms around the house all day, recounting the incident in her mind. When the child comes in from school, mom is still pouting and angry. The atmosphere at the dinner table is tense. Mom isn't speaking to anyone. "Ma'am," I want to ask, "wouldn't it be better to be reconciled and to have a pleasant meal than to be right?"

Reconciliation always involves getting your ego under control and being willing to forego exacting that pound of flesh from the person who slighted you, just to prove you were right. We can't live together in families and society without being willing to forgive and to be reconciled instead of insisting that everyone apologize to us and do *their* part. Jesus said that when someone hurts us, we are to go to them instead of waiting for them to make up with us (see Matt. 5:23–24). Reconciliation often means reaching out and taking the initiative to rebuild the relationship, even when we weren't in the wrong.

Get Things in Perspective

If being the one to reach out and restore a relationship sounds too hard, think about what took place when God looked at our sins: "While we were still sinners, Christ died for us" (Rom. 5:8). Remembering that he took the first step in trying to restore a relationship with us should help us keep matters in perspective when others sin against us.

secrets of a satisfying life

In fact, the issue of forgiveness among people is based on the nature of God and his forgiveness of us. The incarnation, God's giving of his only Son, is the prototype, the example, of the way you and I ought to be willing to extend forgiveness. And remember, Jesus said that if we don't forgive those who sin against us, neither will our heavenly Father forgive us (Matt. 6:15). Now that motivates me! Knowing that God's nature won't allow him to forgive me unless I forgive others makes me want to *seek* to forgive others instead of sitting on my hands and waiting for others to come to me begging for forgiveness.

Did you know that the Internal Revenue Service had to set up what's called the "Government Conscience Fund"? This fund was established because people's consciences often bother them so much that they seek forgiveness for having previously cheated on their income taxes. The U.S. government takes in millions of dollars each year through this fund. One person sent in $10,000 in the form of 100 crisp $100 bills. Another person sent in the small sum of $15.43 because this was the outstanding balance owed from an old court case. Both actions reflected what many people do annually: they try to quiet their consciences by giving the government what was owed.[1]

Keeping a Sensitive Conscience

It's become popular in many circles these days to protest anything that makes us feel guilty or makes our conscience hurt. Of course, some people have been shamed so much that they have an overactive conscience. But God made us so that when we withhold something as valuable as forgiveness from others, our conscience *should* bother us.

I once heard of a man who went to a Christian psychiatrist because he was having a lot of problems in his family. "Doc," he said, "I have a lot of issues at home, especially with my wife. It involves the way I've been dabbling in sin, and my conscience is making me sick. Can you give me anything for it?"

And the doctor said, "You mean you want help in stopping your sinful behavior?"

"Oh no!" the man replied. "I want to know how to stop my conscience from bothering me!"

Unlike this man, Jesus *is* concerned about our consciences. He's concerned that we keep our consciences from being seared, rendering us unfeeling and indifferent. This is especially crucial in the context of the family. If we are walking on eggshells at home because we're not being open and honest with our spouses, we don't need someone to dull our conscience; we need to come clean!

We're under tremendous pressure these days to develop the ability to live at odds with what we believe. From many sources come voices that ask us to change our philosophy of life, our view of what's right and wrong, so that living wrong doesn't disturb us so much. Part of this is because of the universal tendency to avoid the pain and pangs of conscience. Don't give in to this pressure. The crucible of the disturbed conscience is where we forge a values system that enables us to line up the way we live with what is right and to maintain a harmonious relationship not only with family members but also with God.

Stop Playing the Blame Game

Another way we can let go of the past and become more forgiving is to stop shifting the blame away from our own attitudes and actions and placing it elsewhere.

I remember the story of the Quaker who tried his best to live a nonviolent life, as his faith had prescribed. One night he heard a noise upstairs. When he went up to investigate, he saw a thief rummaging through his belongings. The Quaker ran down to the basement and got the shotgun he kept for shooting varmints on his farm. He ran back upstairs, pointed the gun at the thief, and said, "Sir, I am a peaceful man, but I must warn thee that thou art standing where I am about to shoot!"

Of course, this is no worse than the way we try to rearrange the furniture of our minds in order to shift the blame for our evil intent and unforgiving spirits to others. Working through the hurts that arise when people try to live in community with each other is often painful. Admitting our own mistakes can be particularly painful, especially admitting those that may have led to the problem. It often seems easier to blame the other person and leave it at that than to approach the issue directly and work through the problem. But a festering spiritual wound can spread a deadly infection. Accepting responsibility and dealing with the issue directly is both healthier and right. The blame game is not constructive and should be stopped, but that's not an easy thing to do. Yet God gives the needed measure of faith to those who ask.

Released to Look to the Future

Forgiveness releases us to look to the future instead of being oriented toward the past. Forgiveness empowers us to be the people we were destined to be.

I wonder whether you are ensnared behind the prison walls of an unforgiving spirit even as you read these lines. You may be outwardly free, walking around as though you are liberated, but your spirit can still be imprisoned. If this is the case with you, then you're trapped in the past, confined to a prison that is largely of your own making.

God has not destined you to live in prison! He has foreordained you to be free of every part of your past that has allowed an unforgiving spirit to imprison you. Can you, in faith, muster up the courage and the spiritual energy to simply say, "Lord, I forgive my husband"? Can you forgive your wife, or your mother, or your father, or your boss, or anyone else who has held you captive to feelings of bitterness and resentment all this time? Can you simply say, "God, I ask you for the faith and the grace and the mercy to let them go"?

If you can, imagine now the future that will unfold before you! You'll be able to live in the power to help your family become more pleasing to God. You'll be able to change the atmosphere at your job. You'll be able to become the man or woman God's called you to be.

When you let go of all the ugliness that's been done to you in the past, you'll begin to look like a true member of God's family. Remember that one of your heavenly Father's greatest traits is the power to forgive—so much so that "he gave his one and only Son, that whoever believes in him shall not perish but have eternal life" (John 3:16). He has freed you from living in bondage to an unforgiving spirit. And now, as you offer forgiveness to those who sin against you, you're taking on the character of your heavenly Father.

Isn't all this worth far more than clinging to the past that has enslaved you?

secrets of a satisfying life

10

joining the happy breed

Behavioral scientists have learned that people who live their lives by a set of strongly held religious beliefs are far more satisfied with their lives than those living without faith. These strongly held beliefs help in answering difficult questions that would otherwise disturb our comfortable lives.

A survey by the Gallup Organization concluded that fewer than 10 percent of Americans are deeply committed Christians. But the people comprising this group, according to Gallup, can be categorized as particularly influential and happy. Labeling them "a breed apart," Gallup noted that this group is more tolerant of people of diverse backgrounds, more involved in charitable activities, and committed to prayer. As a deeply committed Christian, I draw answers from the Bible, paying particular attention to the philosophical question that baffles so many unhappy people: "Why did

God let this happen?" Finding a defensible answer will help to set you apart as a member of the "happy breed."

Tackling the Problem of Pain

Pain is no respecter of persons. It hits everyone—happy and unhappy people alike. Bad things happen to good people, whatever your definition of good may be. And bad things happen to bad people, whatever your definition of bad may be. The question that most often comes to mind when pain hits us is, why me? And others around us also pose the question, why did God let this happen? People present these questions to me regularly. And I must admit that some things that happen are extremely perplexing, paradoxical, and confusing. In any given week in my position as a pastor to more than five thousand people, I am faced with crises for which there are absolutely no words.

What do you say to someone grappling with the pain of betrayal, divorce, miscarriage, or death? No creative strategies help console people who are in the clutches of bona fide pain. Yet I have learned that trying to answer "Why me?" or "Why did God let this happen?" is unproductive. Rather, the question we should explore is this: "How do you move away from the pain?" Pain is not always bad. It has the power of spurring us into action. It helps us navigate the often-stormy sea of life and produce a better tomorrow. In Romans 5:3–4, the apostle Paul says: "Not only so, but we also rejoice in our sufferings, because we know that suffering produces perseverance; perseverance, character; and character, hope."

Hope is one of God's prescriptions to remedy tragedy, unbearable pain, and emotional and psychological confusion. Although hope is readily available, it is often overlooked until pain becomes unbearable. In his book *The Problem of Pain*, noted philosopher C. S. Lewis writes, "God whispers to us in our pleasures, speaks in our consciences, but shouts in our pains. It is his megaphone to rouse a deaf world."[1] Like a double-edged sword, pain brings excruciating sorrow while at the same time turns our hearts toward the hope God offers. And when we get in touch with pain, we often get in touch with God.

The fields of philosophy and medicine both support the need for pain. Nobel Prize winner George Wald said, "When you have no experience of pain, it is rather hard to experience joy."[2] Some scientists say that pain is a human warning device to alert us to imminent danger or to help us to respond appropriately after we have become the victims of danger. Dr. Paul Brand, a world-renowned expert on leprosy and a medical doctor at the leprosarium in Carville, Louisiana, received a multi-million-dollar grant for the purpose of designing an artificial pain system. He knew that people with diseases such as leprosy and diabetes were in grave danger of losing fingers, toes, and even entire limbs because their warning system of pain had been silenced.[3]

Despite the obvious benefits of pain, every adult alive has at some point posed the question, either rhetorically or in prayerful despair, *Where is God when it hurts?* I raise this question not to question the goodness of God or to point the finger of blame in his direction. Rather, I pose the question to help us seek God's presence and help during painful ordeals. Instead of focusing on the reasons why God allows pain, I am inviting you to explore the more practical question of how we can see God through the pain we experience. Here we are no longer asking "Why?" but instead "What can we do when faced with pain?" The *why* question doesn't provide us with an answer; it only brings up other paradoxical questions that lead to continued dissatisfaction with life and God.

Jesus's Answer to "Where Is God When It Hurts?"

Perhaps you have experienced a tragedy in your own life that caused you to ask the question, "Where is God when it hurts?"[4] Some people in Jesus's day confronted him with a similar question, as recorded in the book of Luke:

> Now there were some present at that time who told Jesus about the Galileans whose blood Pilate had mixed with their sacrifices. Jesus answered, "Do you think that these Galileans were worse sinners than all the other Galileans because they suffered this way? I tell you, no! But unless you repent, you too will all perish. Or those eighteen who died when the tower in Siloam fell on them—do you think they were more guilty than all the others living in Jerusalem? I tell you, no! But unless you repent, you too will all perish."
>
> Luke 13:1–5

These five verses highlight a paradox that has perplexed religious communities down through the centuries. This passage shows that the people of Jesus's day often considered sin or wrongdoing to be the cause for suffering. Jesus cited two separate tragedies to provide a full scope of human suffering. In the first scenario, the wicked governor Pilate had a number of Galileans slaughtered mercilessly while they were participating in worship. The second scenario was the public tragedy of eighteen construction workers who died when the tower they were erecting in Siloam accidentally fell on them. Yet Jesus quickly discounted the victims' sins as the reason for their untimely deaths. On

secrets of a satisfying life

the surface, his response, "I tell you, no! But unless you repent, you too will all perish" (vv. 3, 5), doesn't seem to apply. However, when you dissect Jesus's comment, you will discover four answers to the practical question of where God is when we are hurting. The answers hidden in this passage are: (1) tragedy should shock the careless; (2) pain is a wake-up call; (3) hope in the future; and (4) pain is a call to repentance.

Tragedy Should Shock the Careless

Whenever Jesus spoke, his advice had at least two meanings: the surface understanding and the deeper message. The latter meaning is intended to transform the hearer's actions and moral foundation. Jesus's words, "But unless you repent, you too will all perish" (Luke 13:3), offer a profound message that relates a present situation to an eternal perspective.

In this case, Jesus helps his hearers realize that tragedy should shock the careless because anyone—good or bad—can slip into eternity as a result of an unexpected misfortune. This was the case for the Galilean worshipers and for the eighteen construction workers who slipped into eternity because of a sudden catastrophe. Onlookers or hearers of such tragic news should allow this pain to remind them of the brevity of life and the role of God. If you are someone who is careless or unmindful of God and eternity, you should be shocked into sensible living by such painful calamities. Moses prayed for us to pattern our lives this way when he wrote, "Teach us to number our days aright, that we may gain a heart of wisdom" (Ps. 90:12). This familiar verse is often used by clergy during eulogies. It moves the hearers to a place of keen awareness because their loved ones may have been snatched away suddenly.

Several years ago a tragedy struck the community of Montclair, New Jersey, where my congregation has been based since 1994. A local police officer who had been estranged from his wife went back home, and the couple began to talk. Soon an argument ensued, and the policeman drew his service revolver and killed his wife. To make matters worse, he then turned the gun on himself.

Since the wife and her college-aged daughter had been frequent visitors of our church, the double funeral was to be held there. Our pastoral team knew how futile it would be to tell the daughter, who was left to deal with the tragic loss of both her parents, about the reasons for suffering. Such moments are not a time for explanations, no matter how well intentioned they may be. Rather, these painful moments are times for embracing the sufferers and assuring them that they are loved and valued. Our congregation simply opened the doors of the church to this young woman and her extended family. Our pastoral team and church family also opened the doors of our hearts to assist them during this painful time. As a result, those who came to the service not only left thinking about the brevity of their own lives but also were made aware of the role that God plays in painful moments.

Pain Is a Wake-Up Call

Let's take another look at Jesus's response to the question of where God is when we are hurting: "But unless you repent, you too will all perish" (Luke 13:3). While pain certainly shocks the careless, simply being shocked may not motivate them to make a change for the better. Inherent in Jesus's response is a second, more penetrating answer—a wake-up call. The phrase "wake-up call" connotes that a person needs outside assistance to wake up from a sound sleep. In giving his answer, Jesus realized that this group questioning him was not merely seeking truth but wanted to stir up an intellectual challenge meant to mislead and to discredit his authority. But Jesus, the master philosopher and chief theologian, gave them a real zinger—an answer that served as a wake-up call regarding the destiny and welfare of their souls. In essence, Jesus was saying to the crowd, "If you really want to experience the pain of unsuspecting tragedy, imagine perishing without repentance." He was urging them to focus on being prepared for eternity—with or without God. Jesus wanted to free them from the natural response of getting bogged down in faultfinding concerning this type of tragedy. He was redirecting their focus toward the power of presence.

The Power of Presence

In 1996, members of a local gang viciously attacked a rival gang, killing a youngster who lived in Montclair, the town where our church is located. His family held his wake and funeral at a well-known funeral home in town. Since his family did not attend our church, I was quite surprised to receive a call from the town's police chief, who requested that I attend this funeral dressed in clerical attire. The police chief didn't want me to deliver the eulogy. Instead, my function was to simply sit there as conspicuously as possible, decked out in my black suit and formal white clerical collar. That day I understood the power of presence.

The chief of police wanted members of the local clergy to create an atmosphere where funeral attendees—other gangbangers—would know that their behavior was under the watchful eye of God's representatives, the preachers. Our vestments publicly conveyed that any action that went against mourning and eulogizing was unacceptable and could jeopardize the welfare of their souls. In essence, we were there to offer an official wake-up call against any further violence or retaliation. The chief's suggestion worked. No shootout occurred that day, nor was any violence in any way connected to the death of the young man reported following the funeral.

Similarly, Jesus's response was aimed at getting the crowd to think about eternity in a very sober way. Therefore, a plausible answer to the question of where God is when it hurts is this: wake up and focus on the eternal resting place of your soul.

Living Soberly

Several years ago I was called to deliver a eulogy at the funeral of a little girl who was only about a year old. I sat with the parents as we wept and shared intimate thoughts we never would have shared apart from this tragedy. Here was a baby who had not yet walked, had not learned to read or to say "I love you, Mommy and Daddy," yet she was gone. The three of us sat together vacillating between thanking God that this little life was now with him and lamenting that she had not experienced more of this life.

Psalm 116:15 says, "Precious in the sight of the LORD is the death of his saints." I affirm that the feelings we share at such moments are very precious. Although they do not give an adequate *reason* for the untimely death of our loved ones, our emotions are precious nonetheless. After a few months of helping the parents of that one-year-old child work through the grief process, a bond of spiritual intimacy was formed between us that never would have been established without God's power to create a fellowship out of suffering.

After our meetings I would rush home to hug my daughters. "Dad, what are you doing?" they'd ask. Or they'd complain that I had squeezed them too tightly. With tears in my eyes, I'd say, "I just love the way you smell" or "I just want you to know how much I love you." During that time period I'd even catch myself squeezing the arm of friends and colleagues a bit longer than usual. I sincerely wanted them to know how much I cared about them before it was too late. The tragedy I was helping this couple deal with became my own wake-up call.

Where is God when it hurts? He is very present among us in allowing us to truly treasure the moments we have with our loved ones. Let your pain wake you up!

Hope in the Future

The people who questioned Jesus were asking him about an event that had occurred in the past. Although Jesus did not directly answer their questions, his response added a new dimension to their perspectives about life and how one ought to deal with suffering. He urged them to allow the tragedies that had happened to wrench their attention away from the past and toward the future. He showed them how to hope in the future. Their immediate need to repent was far greater than their need to understand what had happened in the past.

In the absence of a society that still faces the problem of evil, Scripture points us to a future in which evil will be conquered by good. For example, note how the apostle Paul shifts our focus from his present reality of pain toward a glorious future with God when he says, "I consider that our present sufferings are not worth comparing with the glory that will be revealed in us" (Rom. 8:18). Although we are not given a detailed description of the future, we are promised *a future*. And the promise of a future translates into hope.

This is what I had to emphasize as I sat in the hospital room of a woman who had just suffered her fifth miscarriage. I urged her to accept the fact that God would heal her suffering and pain if she would just give him *time*. I tried to convince her not to allow the bitterness of her present pain to consume her and to obscure her faith in God and his promise of a future for her. I tried to convey hope even while she was facing the pinnacle of her pain, telling her that in time, hope would settle in as her best friend, one that would comfort her through all of her troubles.

The Future Can Be Our Friend

My wife and I personally experienced this dimension of shared pain several years ago. I was at home on a Friday afternoon, preparing for my Sunday sermon. My wife, Marlinda, called at about noon from the doctor's office. She said that she hadn't been feeling well and had decided to pay the doctor a visit. "Honey, guess what?" she said.

"I can't guess," I answered.

"The doctor says I'm pregnant!" Marlinda exclaimed.

As the parents of two teenage girls, we had always dreamed of having a boy. So naturally my mind was flooded with images of playing football with "David Jr." Then Marlinda said that she was scheduled to see the doctor again in about three hours. That didn't sound quite right to me, and I remember falling silent for a moment. With excitement still in her voice, Marlinda told me she was going to have lunch before the appointment and that she would call me back after that.

Can you imagine trying to study for a Sunday sermon while you're waiting for such an important call? When the phone finally rang, it was Marlinda, and she was in tears. "I just had a miscarriage," she said. I rushed to the doctor's office to be with her, and we fell into each other's arms. Only a few hours earlier we had shared the idea of the birth of a child, and now those dreams were shattered. Yet we could still *share our pain*, leaning on and comforting each other because we had a common need to stand together in the midst of our suffering.

In the case of my wife's miscarriage, we were certain that the "answer" to our suffering was not in that hospital; it was in the future that God had planned for us. We took comfort in the loving family we already had and in how much more we would work to keep our relationship healthy.

As you read these words, if you are hurting, make up your mind that you will not dwell in the quicksand of your pain. Don't stay bogged down in the present, wrestling with the anguish and hardship of your hurt and misunderstanding. Look ahead! Look forward! Get up from here! Move on! Life still continues. Realize that the future is your friend.

Stop Blaming and Start Living

In our pain and anger, we naturally want to find something or someone to "pin it on." You can blame God, you can blame your spouse, you can blame the government, or you can blame your employer. You can even blame your pain on the impersonal "injustice." But what good does that do? How much better it is to recognize that life is sometimes unfair, but life is also short and our hurts are finite—whereas God's future is forever.

This is why Jesus turned the thoughts of those who questioned him from the *why* of those who had suffered to the *what* concerning things they would do with their own lives. What if their lives were cut short just as the lives of those they asked about were? This is why the apostle Paul reminds us that "our light and momentary troubles are achieving for us an eternal glory that far outweighs them all. So we fix our eyes not on what is seen, but on what is unseen. For what is seen is temporary, but what is unseen is eternal" (2 Cor. 4:17–18).

Pain is only temporary. Its effects may last a year, ten years, twenty years, or a lifetime. But the attitude we have toward God, despite our pain, lasts forever. The psalmist puts it this way: "weeping may remain for a night, but rejoicing comes in the morning" (Ps. 30:5).

Pain Is a Call to Repentance

Because Jesus's questioners were "people of the Covenant," they had been taught that God would bless the faithful and punish the wicked. Over the long haul, this is a fair interpretation of the "covenant theology" outlined in the book of Deuteronomy (see Deut. 28:1–19). It says that when you "fully obey the LORD your God and carefully follow all his commands I give you today" (Deut. 28:1), God promises to bless you. But "if you do not obey the LORD your God" (Deut. 28:15), you will be cursed.

By Jesus's day, however, this promise had been reduced to a "deal" with God. Every time someone suffered, people had the tendency to automatically conclude that the sufferer had done wrong. And any time they saw a wealthy man, they thought they could "take it to the bank" that he was righteous. Of course the covenant was never that simplistic. Jesus makes this clear by his "leveling" statement in Luke 13: "Unless you repent, you too will all perish" (v. 5). Here Jesus is simply stating a universal principle that should help us guard against arrogance. Jesus is warning his questioners that *all people* are subject to God's judgment and that even those who think they are righteous are subject to God's law of repentance. *Repentance* is a directional word that speaks of morally turning away from sin or disobedience of God's laws and moving toward a new position of righteous and godly living. Jesus is saying that even righteous people are susceptible to sudden tragedy and that they too need to live with an attitude of repentance.

A pastor friend of mine took a trip from Augusta, Georgia, to nearby Atlanta to visit his adult daughter. He checked into a hotel, where he had planned to stay for the duration of his visit. One morning when the hotel's housekeeping staff came to clean the room, they discovered my friend dead in his bed. He was in his late forties and knew of no health problems. This was a righteous man, a man of integrity, who was cut down in his prime.

Even Jesus experienced separation from God, a kind of "perishing," as he hung on the cross. "*Eloi, Eloi, lama sabach-thani?*" he cried. "My God, my God, why have you forsaken me?" (Matt. 27:46). Do we think that we, as sinful people, are exempt from experiencing separation from God when the sinless Son of God did so for us? He paid the price so we would not have to be eternally separated from God, despite our sinfulness. He lived in a world in which even he, though sinless, endured the experience of separation from God for a moment. Even if we have a clear conscience, we are not to suppose that we are exempt from God's laws (see 1 Cor. 4:4). We ought to live in an attitude of repentance in response to Jesus's call. No one is exempt.

I am thankful that when we do respond to God in faith and repentance, we have an "insurance policy" against even sins of which we are unaware. The apostle John said that "if we walk in the light, as he [Jesus] is in the light, we have fellowship with one another, and the blood of Jesus, his Son, purifies us from all sin" (1 John 1:7).

The word *purifies* (or *cleanses*) is in the present continuous tense. It means that when we take Jesus seriously and are not too arrogant to repent, God puts us *continuously* in touch with his purifying power. This is the security of being "in Christ." It is recognizing that although you are imperfect, the blood of Jesus keeps you washed and cleansed. But I would not be faithful to Jesus's teaching if I did not remind you that the condition of living in this security is faith and repentance.

I knew a man who went on a twenty-one-day fast. Toward the end of the fast he had a vision. In the vision he saw people walking in hell, screaming because of the flames. One man kept picking up the heads of people and staring at their faces as they burned in the flames. The man who was having the vision asked the Lord what this poor soul was doing. And the Lord said, "He's looking for the preacher who lied to him and told him there was no such thing as perishing in hell!"

Jesus's love for you doesn't exempt you from his universal law: "Unless you repent, you too will perish." And although the experience of pain reminds us of that principle, the pain we experience in this life, no matter how difficult, cannot be compared with that which we will suffer if we die having been too arrogant to repent and accept Christ's salvation.

Closing the Emotional Holes

Jesus's four answers to the question of where God is when it hurts provide a closure to the "what do we do" question surrounding pain. These answers offer a biblical framework to bring closure to the emotional holes that leak hope out of our lives. I have discovered that when someone is wrestling with a philosophical question concerning the absence of God in their pain, Satan's trick is to use that question to keep them in an endless chase for meaning—especially the question of "Why did this happen to me?"

The picture in my mind during these times is one of a dog chasing its tail and thinking that the moment it catches it, happiness will result. Of course the dog never catches its tail. But when it goes about its business, its tail—happiness—follows it. Like the dog chasing its tail, humans will never be able to find a specific answer to the philosophical question "Why did this happen to me?"

However, when the question changes to "How do I move away from the pain?" we find that the power of hope moves us away from a place of despair. Jesus's answers released a sense of hope, which results in a closure to the hopelessness of the philosophical search. Accepting this answer, even in part, helps us to join the happy breed—people who find satisfaction and meaning out of life's paradoxes.

11

laugh twice and call me
in the morning

In *The Anatomy of an Illness: As Perceived by the Patient*, Norman Cousins tells of being hospitalized with a rare, crippling disease. When he was diagnosed as incurable, Cousins checked out of the hospital. Aware of the harmful effects that negative emotions can have on the body, Cousins reasoned that the reverse was also true. He decided to borrow a movie projector and prescribe his own treatment consisting of Marx Brothers films and old *Candid Camera* reruns. Before long he discovered that ten minutes of laughter provided two hours of pain-free sleep. Amazingly, his debilitating disease was eventually reversed. After the account of his victory appeared in the *New England Journal of Medicine*, Cousins received more than three thousand letters from appreciative physicians around the world. Developing the practice of laughing at life's circumstances or a humorous joke is a common habit of happy people.[1]

Two years ago we gave out awards at our staff Christmas party. To ensure that all the bases were covered, the traditional awards like "Best Attendance" and "Employee of the Year" were distributed along with awards for the staff members who had the "Greatest Development" and "Offered the Most Encouragement." The one that I really enjoyed giving out was for the person who had the "Funniest Laugh." When all the votes were tallied some weeks prior to the party, the winner from among the entire staff was clear. The gentleman has an infectious laugh. When Robbie laughs, everyone who hears him begins to laugh too. His laughter seems so enjoyable to him and to everyone else. His body shakes; the pitch of his voice changes; his smile depicts a true genuineness. It is a sight to behold. Sometimes when I'm around him I say something slightly humorous just to get a laugh out of him. My spirit picks up, and I leave the room feeling lighter. I am then able to embrace a new perspective that says, "David, what you're dealing with is not all that bad. Cheer up!"

The Medicine of Laughter

The Bible is right: "A cheerful heart is good medicine" (Prov. 17:22). This verse is not just a nice pithy statement written by Solomon to justify his use of court jesters to entertain him. Nor is it a cliché we preachers use to support our pulpit humor. Medical and sociological data exists to underscore how laughter contributes to a person's happiness.

University of Iowa Health Science Relations and associate professor of internal medicine Nicole Nisly, M.D., observes that "Laughter recently got a boost when research-ers announced at an American Heart Association meeting last November [2002] that heart-healthy people are more likely to laugh frequently and heartily than those with heart disease."[2] Nisly adds that although we do not know the full extent of laughter's contribution to health, the medical evidence suggests that laughter may result in a reduction of stress hormones, leading to a reduction in blood pressure. This in turn may reduce the risk of heart disease.

Laughter has also been found to decrease tension and reduce pain. Laughter appears to boost the body's produc-tion of infection-fighting antibodies. It also has the potential to help in the treatment of depression and other emotional illnesses.[3] Laughter is medicinal to the human soul. Imagine your physician writing you a prescription that reads, "Laugh twice and call me in the morning." You would probably do a double-take when you read the form. I caution you, however, don't be too cynical. It really works.

The Gift of Laughter

A recent trip to my neighborhood video rental store taught me a valuable lesson. As I stood in the checkout line with my DVD, I couldn't help overhearing the spirited conversa-tion occurring near me between a mother and her teenage daughter. The mother wanted to rent a comedy, while the daughter wanted to rent a movie from the drama category. The daughter was pretty clear about her disapproval of her mother's choice of film. "I don't see the point in watching a comedy. You laugh, and it's all over. Nothing has changed," she said. The mother, however, did not want to take the time to justify her movie choice. Perhaps the argument would have gone on for a while if the mother wasn't insistent. But

I believe I know the mom's reason: she needed the medicine that laughter provides. The daughter couldn't see it. Maybe she had not lived long enough to grapple with the stress and pressures of life. These challenges drive a person to God's pharmaceutical store for an over-the-counter supply of laughter pills.

God gave humanity the gift of laughter. The ancient Hebrew people understood that and exercised hearty laughter during times of God's deliverance. Psalm 126 offers a wonderful illustration of the role of laughter in the lives of the Old Testament saints. Please give this song that was written to draw people upward toward God a fresh read.

> When the LORD brought back the captives to Zion,
>   we were like men who dreamed.
> Our mouths were filled with laughter,
>   our tongues with songs of joy.
> Then it was said among the nations,
>   "The LORD has done great things for them."
> The LORD has done great things for us,
>   and we are filled with joy.
> Restore our fortunes, O LORD,
>   like streams in the Negev.
> Those who sow in tears
>   will reap with songs of joy.
> He who goes out weeping,
>   carrying seed to sow,
>   will return with songs of joy,
>   carrying sheaves with him.

Three of the primary reasons laughter can be seen as a medicine to the soul of humanity are exemplified here in Psalm 126. The practice of laughter became a habit because it was exercised in a widespread manner when (1) dreams were fulfilled, (2) people cherished their relationship with God, and (3) people experienced a satisfying life.

Laugh When Your Dreams Are Fulfilled

The Israelites considered themselves as "men who dreamed" when the Lord brought them back from captivity to the city of Zion, their homeland. Whether it was the freedom from over four hundred years of slavery in Egypt, the overthrow of the Midianites by Gideon and his men, or the deliverance from despotic rulers, the awakened sense of sight, sound, smell, and emotions of being released from captivity to return back home could only be expressed in joyful laughter. Every Hebrew dreamed of this day. The freedom from bondage was good, but the idea of returning home to enjoy that freedom elicited another whole set of feelings that could not fully be described, even by poets and songwriters. Oh, how I wish I could have been there to see the people laughing and dancing because their dreams were fulfilled! Although I cannot go back to the times of antiquity, the same experience is still available today.

Oftentimes we don't experience the word picture "Our mouths were filled with laughter, our tongues with songs of joy" (Ps. 126:2) because we have become too battle-fatigued to celebrate with a hearty laughter that overshadows the pain of our past experiences. Celebration is a habit you must learn. Victory from pain deserves an enduring laugh. Can you remember when your freedom and deliverance from a painful trial seemed like only a dream? Well, now that you have been freed, laugh! And if you're still in the battle, make a decision today that once God returns you to Zion—the place of praise—you are going to have a laughing fit. Promise yourself that pleasure! Then sit back and watch how God will plan your comeback, as he did for the Hebrew people.

Laugh Because You Cherish Your Relationship with God

The psalmist was emphatic that the return of the captives to Zion was solely attributed to God. *He* had brought them back, not Moses, or Gideon, or some other human agent. The use of the word *Zion* rather than Jerusalem, Judah, or Israel to depict the place they were returned to highlights the reason why their laughter was so important. Although Zion was just a hill on the north side of the city of Jerusalem, it was of great importance because it was the location of the temple. The returned captives cherished their reconnection with God's house because it was a sign of the genuineness of their repentance from sin and God's subsequent redemptive act of bringing them back to *his* house. The response of the freed people was to proclaim how their mouths were filled with laughter.

I cannot prove the following statement conclusively, but I honestly believe that my congregation's hearty laughter during our Sunday services is a sign of their spiritual health. I am not referring to the laughing at silly jokes, witty comments, or the normal flubs that they witness during public events. Instead, I am referring to the laughter that breaks out at announcements that God's deliverance has occurred in the lives of others—at the testimonies of the return of prodigal sons and daughters or of the fulfillment of God's promises to our church. I believe these are a true reason for congregational celebration that is evidenced by laughter and singing.

When people truly cherish their personal relationship with the Lord, they are free to express every emotion in the presence of others of the same precious faith. The expression of laughter in Psalm 126 resulted in the international broadcasting of the testimony of God's blessings upon his people. The psalmist wrote, "Then it was said among the nations, 'The LORD has done great things for them'" (v. 2). Other nations heard about God's power partly because of the sustained laughter and rejoicing going on at Zion.

How about you? Can you honestly say, "The Lord has done great things for me, and I am filled with joy"? Making this affirmation is an indicator of where you are spiritually. Some people know intuitively and from experience that God is good, but they are silent regarding their appreciation of the impact of this goodness on their lives. The contrasting personality is the one who knows that God is good and dares not hold back the expression of their appreciation. If God has been good to you, tell it! Rather, break out in laughter so that others may hear of his goodness.

Laugh When You Experience a Satisfying Life

A satisfying life is one that bounces back from tragedy, pain, or disappointment. A satisfied life is not one that never experiences bumps in the road. Satisfaction is the feeling that emerges from overcoming something that could bring dissatisfaction. The psalmist explains this transition from tragedy to triumph by stating, "Those who sow in tears will reap with songs of joy. He who goes out weeping, carrying seed to sow, will return with songs of joy, carrying sheaves with him" (Ps. 126:5–6).

Charles Haddon Spurgeon, the famed English preacher, comments on these two verses by writing, "This promise is conveyed under images borrowed from the instructive scenes of agriculture. In the sweat of his brow the husbandman tills his land, and casts the seed into the ground, where for a time it lies dead and buried. A dark and dreary winter succeeds, and all seems to be lost; but at the return of spring universal nature revives, and the once desolate fields are covered with corn which, when matured by the sun's heat, the cheerful reapers cut down, and it is brought home with triumphant shouts of joy."[4]

This Bible passage is informing us of the cyclical nature of satisfaction. Satisfaction follows dissatisfaction. If you have found yourself embroiled in dissatisfaction, rejoice because satisfaction is about to be harvested. It comes to you as it does to the farmer who brings home the crops *after* sowing in tears. The role of laughter in this cyclical process is to carry you through the periods where things look bleak. This cycle is a principle. Principles work regardless of emotions, feelings, or personal sentiments. The farmer reluctantly takes the few seeds, which he would rather use to feed his family, to plant the crop for the following year's harvest. He knows instinctively that the principle of sowing and reaping always works. Likewise, you should know that laughter sustains us during times of dissatisfaction and that satisfaction follows dissatisfaction. Don't wait until the battle is over—laugh now!

Laughter is a habit that happy people have incorporated into their lives because they realize that this approach is one of the secrets to attaining a satisfying life. What alternative exists that offers the medical, psychological, and spiritual benefits that the habit of laughter delivers? We are hard pressed to find one. This is why I offer this final prescription to the person seeking to achieve a satisfying life: laugh twice and call me in the morning. In the morning you will feel better. You will recover from the place of defeat.

secrets of a satisfying life

epilogue

Throughout this book I have presented secrets to a satisfying life that can be habit forming. Incorporating a new habit in your life may seem hard at first, but if you can consistently do it for a few weeks, it will become second nature to you.

Recently my trainer was showing me how to do "bicycles," an exercise for firming up the abdomen. At first lying there on my back while moving my feet as if I were pedaling a bicycle seemed so difficult. The problem wasn't just moving my feet up and down in a circular motion; the difficulty was intensified when I was instructed to add another motion to the exercise. My trainer told me to interlock my fingers and put my hands behind my head. Then I had to touch my moving knees, right elbow touching left knee and left elbow touching the right knee. The first time I did this, I thought that my trainer was insane. *There's no way I can do this*, I thought. But sure enough, in a few weeks, I was a bicycle pro.

If I can do the bicycle exercise habitually, you can implement these secrets to a satisfying life in such a way that they become habits. Go for it! It's God's will that you achieve a satisfying life. I look forward to seeing you among the members of the happy breed.

notes

Introduction: The Search for Happiness

1. Quoted in a sermon by Charles A. Jones III, "It's All a Matter of Attitude," First Presbyterian Church, St. Petersburg, FL, June 20, 2004, http://fpc-stpete.org/Sermons2004/June2004.htm.

2. Bernard Rimland, "The Altruism Paradox," *Psychological Reports* 51 (1982): 521.

3. Ibid.

4. Viktor E. Frankl, *Man's Search for Meaning* (New York: Simon & Schuster, 1984), 135.

5. Esther Quintero Cartagena, Ana Diaz, Marviliz Avila, Hilda Burgos, "Client's Opinion about the Use of Humor as a Therapeutic Intervention Strategy," Association for Applied and Therapeutic Humor, September 2005, www.aath.org/articles/art_carta gena.html.

Chapter 1: The Value of Perspective

1. Paul Lee Tan, *Encyclopedia of 7,700 Illustrations* (Garland, TX: Bible Communications, Inc., 1996), Logos Bible Software CD-ROM.

2. Daniel Goleman, *Working with Emotional Intelligence* (New York: Bantam Books, 2000), 54.

3. Gary L. McIntosh and Samuel D. Rima, *Overcoming the Dark Side of Leadership* (Grand Rapids: Baker, 1997), 143.

4. Aleksandr Solzhenitsyn, *The Gulag Archipelago* (New York: HarperCollins, 1973).

5. Jac J. Müeller, *The New International Commentary on the New Testament: The Epistle of Paul to the Philippians* (Grand Rapids: Eerdmans, 1991), 146.

6. William J. Cousins and Paul Oren, "Habit-Ways: A Footnote to Sumner," *Social Forces* 25, no. 4 (May 1947): 417.

Chapter 2: Happy Habits

1. Ed Denier and Martin E. Seligman, "Very Happy People," *American Psychological Society* 13, no. 1 (January 2002): 81–84.

2. This book *Christus Victor*, first published in 1931 and now out of print, is an interpretation of the doctrine of the atonement by Gustav Aulen (New York: Macmillan, 1975).

3. Gail Sheehy, *New Passages: Mapping Your Life Across Time* (New York: Random House, 1995).

4. Bob Wischnia and Paul Carrozza, "Running with President Bush," *Runner's World*, July 2005. Available online at http://www.runnersworld.com/footnotes/gwbush/20questions.html.

Chapter 3: Learning How to Be Satisfied

1. Allen Parducci, *Happiness, Pleasure, and Judgment: The Contextual Theory and Its Applications* (Mahwah, NJ: Erlbaum, 1995).

2. Tan, *Encyclopedia of 7,700 Illustrations.*

3. David D. Ireland, *Perfecting Your Purpose* (New York: Warner-Faith, 2005).

Chapter 4: The Happy, Hopeful Perspective

1. Kevin Johnson, "Ruth Sender: Writer Reveals the Power of Hope," International Education and Resource Network, May 30, 1996, http://www.iearn.org/hgp/aeti/1994-ruth-sender.html.

2. Nerella Ramanaiah and Fred Detwiler, "Life Satisfaction and the Five-Factor Model of Personality," *Psychological Reports* 80 (1997): 1208.

3. Tan, *Encyclopedia of 7,700 Illustrations.*

4. Albert Morehead and Loy Morehead, eds., *The New American Webster Handy College Dictionary*, 3rd ed. (New York: Penguin Putnam, 1995).

5. Barbara Held, "The Tyranny of the Positive Attitude in America: Observation and Speculation," *Journal of Clinical Psychology* 58, no. 9 (2002): 965–92.

6. Ibid.

7. Quoted in Frank Gaebelein, ed., *The Expositor's Bible Commentary* (Grand Rapids: Zondervan, 1976), 10:154.

8. Karen Hammerness, "Learning to Hope, or Hoping to Learn," *Journal of Teacher Education* 54, no. 1 (January/February 2003): 45.

9. Quoted in Tan, *Encyclopedia of 7,700 Illustrations.*

10. Stanley Marcus, *Minding the Store* (Denton, TX: University of North Texas Press, 1981).

11. E. Mavis Hetherington and John Kelly, *For Better or For Worse: Divorce Reconsidered* (New York: W. W. Norton and Company, 2002), 6.

12. The Office of Consumer Affairs, "December 1997 Report on DOC Consumer-Related Information," http://www.library.unt.edu/gpo/oca/mrdec97.htm.

Chapter 5: Living Your Dream

1. Kate Coscarelli, "A Second Calling: Lawyer Becoming a Monk, Four Decades after Ruling Out Priesthood," *Sunday Star-Ledger*, September 1, 2002.
2. SermonNotes.com, "Illustration on Purpose," April 2005, http://www.sermonnotes.com/members/deluxe/illus/p.htm.
3. James S. Hewett, ed., *Illustrations Unlimited* (Wheaton: Tyndale, 1988), 19–20.
4. SermonNotes.com, "Illustration on Adversity," March 2005, http://www.sermonnotes.com/members/deluxe/illus/p.htm.
5. SermonNotes.com, "Illustration on Purpose," April 2005, http://www.sermonnotes.com/members/deluxe/illus/p.htm.

Chapter 6: Happiness and Busyness: Strange Bedfellows

1. Robert Emmons and Henry Kaiser, "Goal Orientation and Emotional Well-Being: Linking Goals and Affect Through Self," in L.L. Martin and A. Tesser (eds.) *Striving and Feeling: Interactions among Goals, Affect, and Self-Regulation* (Mahwah, NJ: Erlbaum, 1996).
2. R. Bailey and C. Miller, "Life Satisfaction and Life Demands in College Students," *Social Behavior and Personality* 26 (1998), 51.
3. Virden Thornton, "The Processionary Caterpillar Syndrome Costs You Sales?" Ezine Articles, April 23, 2005, http://ezinearticles.com/?The-Processionary-Caterpillar-Syndrome-Costs-You-Sales?&id=30434.
4. Hewett, ed., *Illustrations Unlimited*, 277.
5. Ibid., 205.
6. Nadine Stair, "I Would Take More Trips," *Family Circle* 91, no. 4 (March 27, 1978): 99.

Chapter 7: Prescription for Happy Relationships

1. L. Li, D. Young, H. Wei, Y. Zhang, Y. Zheng, S. Xiao, Wang, and X. Chen, "The Relationship Between Objective Life Status and Subjective Life Satisfaction with Quality of Life," *Behavioral Medicine* 23 (1998), 149.
2. S. Sugarman, "Happiness and Population Density" (master's thesis, California State University, 1997).
3. C. Murray and M. J. Peacock, "A Model-Free Approach to the Study of Subjective Well-Being" in *Mental Health in Black America* (Thousand Oaks, CA: Sage, 1996).
4. Ken Sande, *The Peacemaker: A Biblical Guide to Resolving Personal Conflict*, 2nd ed. (Grand Rapids: Baker, 1997).
5. SermonNotes.com, "Illustration on Time," April 2005, http://www.sermonnotes.com/members/deluxe/illus/p.htm.

Chapter 8: Firm Thighs and Sharp Minds

1. J. Gerwood, M. LeBlanc, and N. Piazza, "The Purpose in Life Test and Religious Denomination," *Journal of Clinical Psychology* 54 (1998): 49.
2. Christopher P. Neck, Tedd L. Mitchell, Charles C. Manz, and Emmet C. Thompson, *Fit to Lead* (New York: St. Martin's Press, 2004), 6.

Chapter 9: The Habit of Forgiveness

1. Rick Van Sant, "Guilt-Stricken Pay Up To IRS: 'Conscience Fund' Gets Cash, Quilts," *The Cincinnati Post*, January 26, 1996.

Chapter 10: Joining the Happy Breed

1. C. S. Lewis, *The Problem of Pain* (New York: Simon & Schuster, 1996), 140.

2. George Wald quoted in R. Lanier Britsch and Terrance D. Olson, eds., *Counseling: A Guide to Helping Others* (Salt Lake City: Deseret Book Co., 1983–1985), 1. Available online from LDS Resources on Mental Health, "Counseling: Suffering, Pain and Evil," http://ldsmentalhealth.org/library/mi/milds/milds2001/counseling1/chapter2.htm.

3. Phillip Yancey, *Where Is God When It Hurts?* (Grand Rapids: Zondervan, 1977), 37.

4. As many readers will note, I am indebted for this phrase to the fine book by Phillip Yancey, *Where Is God When It Hurts?*

Chapter 11: Laugh Twice and Call Me in the Morning

1. Norman Cousins, *The Anatomy of an Illness As Perceived by the Patient: Reflections on Healing and Regeneration* (New York: W. W. Norton & Company, 1979).

2. Nicole Nisly, M.D., "Laughter is Medicine from Within," Virtual Hospital, September 2003, http://www.vh.org/adult/patient/internalmedicine/prose/laughter.html.

3. Ibid.

4. Charles H. Spurgeon, *The Treasury of David* (Peabody, MA: Hendrickson Publishers, 1988), 3:77.

Also by David D. Ireland, Ph.D.

Activating the Gifts of the Holy Spirit
Failure Is Written in Pencil
Perfecting Your Purpose
What Color Is Your God?
Why Drown When You Can Walk on Water?

David D. Ireland, Ph.D., is heard nationwide on a daily radio show, *IMPACT with David Ireland*. He is pastor of the five-thousand-member Christ Church in Montclair, New Jersey, which he began in 1986 with six people. He holds degrees in engineering, theology, and organizational leadership.

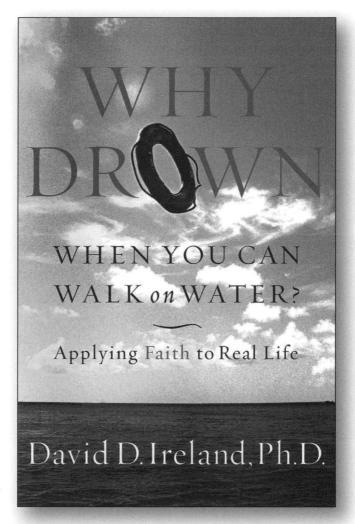